ANTIQUE PISTOLS

An illustrated reference guide
for collectors

Top: Trade label of Parker Field & Sons dating from post 1842 – the year in which William Parker died and his son-in-law took over the business. This style of label was used by a number of makers.

Bottom: Murcott was one of the principal retailers for Colt revolvers. This label is from the case of a 3rd Model Colt Dragoon percussion-cap revolver.

ANTIQUE PISTOLS

An illustrated reference guide for collectors

F. Wilkinson

ARMS AND ARMOUR PRESS
LONDON NEW YORK SYDNEY

To John, Andy, Phil and all the others of "E" District Pistol Club

Published in 1985 by Arms and Armour Press Limited,
2–6 Hampstead High Street, London NW3 1QQ.

Distributed in the USA by Sterling Publishing Co. Inc.,
2 Park Avenue, New York, N.Y. 10016.

Distributed in Australia by
Capricorn Link (Australia) Pty. Ltd., P.O. Box 665,
Lane Cove, New South Wales 2066, Australia.

British Library Cataloguing in Publication Data:
Wilkinson, F. J.
Antique pistols: an illustrated reference guide for collectors. – (Illustrated reference guides for collectors)
1. Firearms I. Title II. Series
683.4 NK6904
ISBN 0-85368-725-0

Designed by David Gibbons; edited by Michael Boxall; typeset by Typesetters (Birmingham) Limited; printed and bound in Great Britain.

Acknowledgments
Unless otherwise stated, all the photographs are of items sold by Sotheby, Parke, Bernet, and the author is grateful for permission to reproduce them.

CONTENTS

INTRODUCTION

Although research has now established that the discovery of gunpowder took place in China as early as the eleventh century, it was to be many centuries before the first practical handgun was developed. The earliest firearm consisted of little more than a tube closed at one end (the barrel), with a hole drilled through the wall near the closed end (the touch hole). The charge of powder was ignited by a glowing ember or the tip of a smouldering match, so that the gun was no more than a simple matchlock. While this system was effective for long arms, it precluded the use of portable weapons which could be carried about the person ready for action. The practical difficulties of coping with the glowing match are obvious.

Late in the fifteenth century or early in the sixteenth, a new system of ignition, the wheel-lock, was developed. This device produced sparks by friction between a piece of naturally occurring mineral, known as pyrites, and the rotating, roughened edge of a steel wheel. To operate the mechanism a key with a square-cut hole, the spanner, was placed over the end of a lug fitted at the centre of the flat wheel. The key was turned and thereby compressed a large V-shaped spring attached to the wheel by a short chain. When the spring was compressed a small, spring-operated arm moved forward to engage the wheel and lock it in place. A piece of pyrites was then placed between the jaws of a pivoted arm, the serpentine, which was then moved forward so that the pyrites pressed against the edge of the wheel. When the trigger was pressed the arm which had locked the wheel was withdrawn permitting the tensioned spring to rotate the wheel rapidly. This movement produced the friction which generated sparks, and as the conjunction of pyrites and wheel was positioned at the base of a pan holding fine grain priming powder this was ignited. The flash from the burning priming passed through the touch hole to ignite the main charge housed in the breech.

The origin of the wheel-lock is unclear, but there seems good reason to think it was quite possibly the brain-child of Leonardo da Vinci, although the earliest recorded reference seems to be in

1515. The town records of Augsburg mention an unfortunate shooting accident involving a young lady and a gallant, and the description of the weapon strongly suggests that it was a wheel-lock.

Since the wheel-lock was mechanically complex it was fairly expensive to manufacture and therefore the early pistols were usually owned by the rich and ruling families of Europe, who not unnaturally demanded top quality pieces. The wheel-lock pistol became a work of art in its own right, with locks and barrels chiselled and stocks inlaid with ivory, horn, mother-of-pearl or steel; the designs often the work of established artists. The majority of early wheel-locks are of German manufacture – especially from Nuremberg and Augsburg. Most conform to a general pattern, with a straight stock and acutely angled butt terminating in a large ball pommel. It has been suggested that the butt was shaped so that when empty the weapon could be used as a club, but this idea has little basis in fact because the majority of ball pommels are fragile and could not have withstood use as a bludgeon. The decorative inlay would also seem to preclude such a crude idea. It is more probably that the large ball was intended to provide an easy means of gripping the butt when drawing the weapon from its holster at the front of a saddle.

The wheel-lock pistol, even when loaded and spanned, was safe. The easiest protection against accidental discharge was to lift the serpentine clear of the pan so that if the wheel slipped and rotated, friction between the pyrites and wheel was impossible and there could be no sparks. The early gunsmiths seem to have been very cautious and many of the lock plates of sixteenth-century wheel-locks are bespotted with projecting studs which operate various safety catches. As the gunsmiths came to realize that these were largely unnecessary they were gradually discarded and this feature can be a useful guide in dating wheel-locks; the more buttons, the earlier the weapon is likely to be.

The wheel-lock remained in use throughout the sixteenth and the first half of the seventeenth centuries, but parallel developments were taking place, and by early in the eighteenth century the wheel-lock was no longer being produced. The principle of mechanical ignition had proved its worth and a similar, but simpler, friction system was being developed. It seems to have had its beginning in northern Europe and is often referred to as the Baltic lock. It consisted of a small arm (the cock), which held, not pyrites, but a piece of flint between adjustable jaws. A simple mechanism provided the motive power to move this arm through an arc. The piece of flint, gripped between the jaws, scraped down the flat face of a vertical steel plate and produced sparks. As the plate was situated above the pan the sparks fell into the priming powder and, via the touch hole, ignited the charge.

The mechanism was, in general, simpler to construct and easier to maintain than the wheel-lock, but there was one small mechanical problem. The priming powder held in the pan needed protection from wind and weather and for this purpose a sliding plate, the pan cover, was fitted across the top of the pan to hold the priming powder safely in place. Before the sparks could fall into the priming obviously the pan cover had to be moved. Early Baltic locks, and a similar system known as the snaphaunce (snaphance), soon evolved a mechanical coupling which ensured that as the cock moved forward the pan cover was automatically pushed clear of the pan. It was realized that this was a rather unnecessary complication and eventually the steel plate and the pan cover were united into one L-shaped piece of metal, generally known among collectors as the frizzen.

The L-shaped frizzen was pivoted at the tip of the short arm so that as the cock flew forward and the flint scraped down the long arm, the frizzen was tipped forward, uncovering the pan and allowing the sparks to ignite the priming. This then was the beginning of what was to prove the most successful, certainly the most long-lived, of all the early mechanical systems of ignition, the flintlock.

The cock was pulled back manually and on the early locks a small pivoted arm or sear protruded through the lock plate to engage with the cock and lock it into the upright position. In 1605 a French maker, Marin Le Bourgeoys, developed a lock in which the projecting sear was dispensed with and the cock was fitted with a flattened metal block (the tumbler) mounted on the inside of the lock plate. Two notches were cut into the edge of the tumbler and an arm (the sear), held under tension by a spring, pressed against the edge of the tumbler. As the cock was pulled back the tumbler was turned until the sear engaged with the first notch. This position, known as half-cock, was safe because the trigger could not disengage the sear and the tumbler was locked. If the cock was pulled further back the sear disengaged from the first notch and slipped into the second from which pressure on the trigger could lift it clear. As the cock was pulled back the mainspring was compressed so that when the tumbler was released from the locking action of the sear the spring pushed the cock forward to initiate the sparking action.

The flintlock was to remain in constant use throughout the seventeenth, eighteenth and a good part of the nineteenth centuries. Naturally over such a long period there were changes in design, and the shape of lock can be a useful guide in dating a flintlock weapon. The earliest locks very much resembled the wheel-lock in shape, with a deep belly to the plate, but gradually the gunsmiths reduced the area of the lock and by the early eighteenth century the lock plate had a slight downward curve giving it a banana shape. This curve gradually reduced and by the end of the century the lock was fairly straight. In similar fashion the shape of the cock altered, and earlier flintlocks have cocks which are flat in section while those of the eighteenth and early nineteenth centuries are usually half-convex in section. The earlier cocks have a very graceful, swan-neck curve which becomes less pronounced as the century progresses. Towards the end of the eighteenth and early in the nineteenth centuries, a flat section, ring-neck cock was adopted with the virtue of simpler construction and greater strength. Triggers too can help in dating; those of the seventeenth century tend to be rather thin and by the end of the seventeenth century and early in the eighteenth century the tip has a backward curl which generally disappears by the 1720s.

Developments were aimed at improving the performance of the lock, and friction was reduced as much as possible by the inclusion of rollers. This was a feature of the later eighteenth and early nineteenth century flintlock, and often a small roller bearing was mounted either on the frizzen spring which holds the frizzen closed or on the tip of the frizzen arm which pressed against the spring. There were also changes in the internal design which reduced friction. The pan which held the priming was very susceptible to rain and to overcome this problem some were so shaped that moisture running down the lock plate would be diverted from the priming itself.

While the French style of lock was probably the most common there were variant forms developed in Spain where the basic action of steel against flint remained unchanged, although the earlier system of sears projecting through the lock plate from the inside continued in use. While the French lock was generally of curved form, the Spanish and Italian variety, known as the Miquelet, had much squarer jaws and in general was much squatter and more rugged in appearance. Variations of the Miquelet lock were produced, but most can be distinguished by the presence of the main spring on the outside of the lock plate. The efficient action of the flintlock very much depended upon the flint and it was generally reckoned that a good-shaped flint would produce thirty good strikings before it was likely to need changing.

Although the flintlock had offered advantages over the wheel-lock it did have certain drawbacks, especially for the hunter. When the trigger was pressed a series of actions was set in motion: the sear was withdrawn from the tumbler; the main spring pushed the cock forward; the flint scraped down the steel face; sparks fell into the priming; this took fire and the flame passed through the touch hole to ignite the main charge and so fire the bullet. Each of these actions took a small but perceptible time so that the sum total was a delay between the pressing of the trigger and the firing of the shot. This hangfire was sufficient to interfere with the aim of the hunter. For a soldier or a target shooter the delay was of no importance because the target was large or stationary, but for the hunter with a moving target it meant that he had to make due allowance for the delay when taking aim – not easy in the field. There was another minor disadvantage in that when the priming flashed it generated a quantity of smoke and flame which might possibly alarm a quarry and give it just that split second's advantage.

Attempts were made to reduce this hangfire and the use of bearings to reduce friction would certainly have helped. A Scottish clergyman from Belhelvie near Aberdeen, produced the answer. Alexander Forsyth was a keen shooter and an amateur chemist who had read of the experiments of an eighteenth-century chemist named Howard with very unstable chemicals known as fulminates which, if struck, exploded. Forsyth endeavoured to speed up the rate of ignition by mixing these fulminates with black powder, but the resulting mixture was not only dangerous but unreliable. Later he developed the idea of using the fulminates to initiate detonation rather than speed up the explosion. He experimented by placing fulminate crystals over the touch hole and then striking them with a metal arm. The resultant flash from the explosion of the fulminates was sufficient to ignite the main charge.

The next problem was how to deposit these crystals at the touch hole in quantities which were small enough to be safe and large enough to ignite the main charge. Forsyth produced a mechanical device, known, because of its shape, as a scent bottle, which was a pivoted metal container holding the fulminate. When rotated through one hundred and eighty degrees the lower section, which held the fulminate, allowed a small number of crystals to fall into, what was in effect, a very small pan by the side of the touch hole. The scent bottle was then returned to its original upright position which now placed a spring-loaded arm, fitted in the upper section, just above the crystals. Forsyth substituted a solid-nosed metal hammer for the cock so that now when the trigger was pressed the hammer swung forward to strike the arm which, in turn, struck the crystals of fulminate to detonate them and ignite the main charge.

The system was rather complex and, to a degree, not very safe; nevertheless it worked and in 1805 Forsyth patented his percussion system. He came to London and set up a shop in Piccadilly to sell his new percussion firearms. Despite some conservative opposition they soon became extremely popular with hunters. This new percussion system simplified the lock since pan, frizzen and frizzen spring were now superfluous and the duration of hangfire was greatly reduced. It offered another advantage in that flintlock weapons could easily be converted to use the new system.

There were numerous attempts to improve the method of depositing the fulminate over the touch hole: it was embedded in wax, placed into the hollow end of quills or fitted in small capsules on to thin pieces of paper. It was not until the 1820s that the most practical and popular system was developed and this was the percussion cap. A small copper thimble had a quantity of fulminate deposited on the inside and it was then pressed over the nipple, a metal tube with a hole drilled through the centre, which led to the touch hole. The friction or 'springyness' of the cap was sufficient to hold it on the nipple. There is some dispute as to who was the original designer or inventor of the percussion cap, but it seems most likely that it was a Joshua Shaw, who patented his device in the United States in 1822. The nose of the hammer was recessed so that as it struck the cap it partially enclosed the nipple and cap so preventing the dangers of fragments of the cap from flying off to strike the shooter in the face.

The use of the percussion cap flourished between the 1820s and the 1850s and was very important in opening the way for the development of a whole range of new firearms. The vast majority of firearms up to this period had been single shot; once the weapon had been discharged it was useless (except as a bludgeon) until re-loaded. There had been multi-shot flintlock weapons, but the necessity for multiple pans and frizzens, or systems which endeavoured to use a single pan and frizzen for a number of barrels, had made development very difficult. However with the percussion cap as a means of ignition these problems were greatly reduced. One of the early forms of multi-shot was the percussion cap pepperbox pistol which was constructed from a single block of metal into which was drilled five of six barrels or chambers, each with its own nipple. This block was mounted so that a single hammer could strike each of the nipples in turn. Some pepper-boxes required the barrels to be rotated by hand, but by the 1830s and 1840s mechanically rotated barrels were commonplace. When the trigger was pulled the cylinder block was rotated, the hammer rose, fell, struck the nipple and fired that barrel; the trigger was now released and pulled again and the action could be repeated until all six shots were fired.

It was in 1835–6 that what was probably the next most significant improvement in firearms design was patented by the American Samuel Colt of Connecticut. Colt certainly did not invent the revolver for there had long been practical revolvers, but what he did was to introduce modern techniques and a very simple but effective system of rotating and locking the cylinder. Despite the novelty of his new design, Colt's incursion into the gun trade was not, at first, very successful. However, thanks largely to the aid and encouragement of a Texas Ranger, Captain Walker, Colt made a fresh start and from them on little went against his best interests. He produced a whole range of popular revolvers including the 1849 Pocket .31 calibre, the .36 Navy and the .44

Army models. In 1851 Colt came to England to display his wares at the Great Exhibition in London. He showed his revolving arms and by shrewd public relations caught the public and official interest and above all created a furore among British makers. Revolver development had been largely overlooked in Europe and the quick, effective action of Colt's revolver was most impressive and represented a great advance in firearms technology. Colt set up a factory in London in 1852–3 and this, of course, irritated and disturbed the English gun trade. This American was encroaching upon their own territory and doing it extremely successfully. This spurred makers such as Robert Adams, William Tranter, James Webley and others to go into revolver production and the middle years of the nineteenth century were rich in revolver designs, some of which were absurd, some very effective.

Many percussion cap revolvers were supplied in wooden cases, usually of oak or mahogany, which held the pistol and the vital accessories such as powder flask, bullet mould, turnscrew, cleaning rods, oil bottles and such other accessories as were required by that particular model of weapon. The system of selling guns in cases had begun late in the eighteenth century when they then normally housed a pair of pistols rather than a single. The lids of most cases were graced by a trade label of the supplier, a feature which is of great help in dating many of these weapons.

The percussion cap was also largely responsible for the introduction of breech-loading weapons, centrefire pistols and revolvers. The wheel-lock, the snaphaunce and the flintlock had all suffered from the handicap of being muzzle loading, that is the charge had to be poured down the barrel from a container, to be followed by the ball which, in turn, had to be pushed home firmly on to the powder. This system of loading was slow and in certain positions, such as prone, could be uncomfortable and difficult. Breech-loading weapons, in which the charge was introduced directly into the breech, had been known since the sixteenth century, but the vast majority of the early examples suffered from poor obturation. This means that because the breech had to be opened to allow the charges to be inserted there was often a gap at the end of the breech. When the charge was fired gas, flame and smoke could well escape through this gap. The gas loss meant less impetus to the bullet which meant less muzzle velocity, shorter range and probably a loss in accuracy. The shooter was also at risk from the escaping gas and flame. The big problem was to devise some means of allowing direct access to the breech and then closing the gap so that gas escape was stopped.

In 1812 Samuel Johannes Pauly had developed a very efficient cartridge with which his breech-loading guns could be loaded, and in essence there is very little difference between the Pauly gun and a modern shotgun. The barrels, pivoted at the breech, could be dropped to allow a cartridge to be inserted into the chamber or breech. The barrels were then closed, the shots were fired, the barrels lowered and the lower section of the cartridge withdrawn. Despite its advanced ideas the gun received little support and was largely ignored. Another step along the road to the modern, self-contained cartridge, was taken in 1835 by Lefaucheux who invented the pinfire cartridge. He produced a metal-cased cartridge which held a charge of powder and a bullet. A small metal pin projected through the side of the case and one end rested on a small primer set in the base. It was loaded into a pistol or revolver which had a slit cut into the breech or cylinder to accommodate the pin. When the trigger was pressed the hammer fell and struck the pin which, in turn, hit the primer to detonate the charge. It was a neat and effective system although a little dangerous since the pins could easily be struck accidentally.

Another development in the history of breech-loading handguns was the Rollin White patent granted in 1855, in which White patented the idea of drilling the chambers right through a revolver's cylinder, which meant that the cylinder could be loaded from the back or the front. In 1856 Daniel Wesson acquired sole rights to this patent and in 1857 Wesson joined Horace Smith; in October of that year Smith & Wesson produced a .22 calibre breech-loading revolver which used a metal cartridge loaded from the rear. In a projecting rim around the base of the cartridge was a small charge of fulminate and when the cartridge was dropped into the chamber the projecting rim rested against the face of the cylinder. The hammer was so designed that when it came down it struck the rim of the cartridge. Since the metal casing was of fairly soft copper the rim was crushed so detonating the fulminate and igniting the charge. This was a tremendous step forward in the development of the revolver and Smith & Wesson held the master patent which prevented their competitors from utilizing this patent until 1869.

At the same time as Smith & Wesson were developing their rimfire revolvers others were exploring the possibilities of another step forward. In the United States Hiram Berdan patented, in 1866, a centrefire cartridge which had a small primer which could be replaced. In Britain, Colonel Boxer was working on the same idea although his primer was of a slightly different design.

By the 1870s the modern revolver and pistol had been developed and the style was set for future developments of semi-automatic handguns and rapid-firing machine-guns.

COLLECTING

If firearms hold the pride of place with arms and armour enthusiasts then certainly pistols hold pride of place among firearms. They are probably popular with more collectors than any other group of weapons. There are several possible explanations not the least of which being that they are generally more available and within a very wide price range. Pistols have been in production from the late sixteenth century until, in collecting terms, the latter part of the nineteenth century, so that the number produced is obviously very high indeed. Pistols were produced in most countries of the world, many with special national features, so the choice is wide.

Early wheel-locks are generally of very high quality and very decorative, but quite rare. This means that their price is obviously going to be very high and it is only a fortunate few that can hope to acquire sixteenth-century wheel-locks. During the seventeenth century they were produced in much plainer and more robust forms and became more widely used by the military so they are less rare, plainer and consequently rather cheaper than earlier examples. However the term cheaper is purely relative and the majority of ordinary wheel-locks of this period are likely to fetch between £1,500 to £2,500 each.

Although wheel-locks are comparatively rare flintlocks are not. They were produced over a period of nearly three centuries from the mid seventeenth to the mid nineteenth, and in most countries of Europe, India, America and Africa, in varying forms and varying sizes. They range from truly superb decorative pieces to the comparatively crude but quite practical pocket pistols, produced in quantity in arms centres such as Liège and Birmingham. It is possible to acquire flintlocks from £80 up to £50,000.

Although percussion weapons were in production for a comparatively shorter period, roughly from the 1820s to 1860s, they were being produced at a time when technology was advancing rapidly and productivity was much higher than it had been. Although percussion-cap weapons are certainly not as popular as flintlocks, there are opportunities for the collector with more limited means to acquire quite a varied range of examples. Rimfire, pinfire and other forms of early cartridge weapons are available in a tremendous variety of shapes and sizes, but their prices vary quite considerably because they fall within a rather grey area in some countries. In Britain until quite recently such weapons were available only to the lucky owners of the appropriate police certificate, but since the latter half of 1984 the regulations have been interpreted more liberally. Rimfire and pinfire weapons, with one or two exceptions, may now be collected without any certificates. This is the general policy, but practice does vary and it is important that local rules be verified. This freedom has brought about a tremendous increase in prices; for example the ordinary pinfire revolver, which a year or two back would have made £10–£15, now will make £60–£80 with corresponding increases for the more desirable pieces.

While collecting pistols can be both rewarding and stimulating a word of warning is necessary. Over the last ten years there has been a very marked increase in the number of replicas, copies or downright fakes. India, Japan and Italy have entered the field of reproducing antique firearms with enthusiasm and skill. Some are produced quite legitimately as modern shooting weapons, others are intended purely as wall decorations but, unfortunately, a number are intended to deceive. The supply of replacement parts has also much increased so that it has become very important for the collector to examine any item very carefully. Unfortunately there are no easy or infallible guide-lines that can be given. As with all fields of collecting, experience and knowledge are the only safeguards and these are not acquired easily. For the beginner the answer is probably to purchase from sources which can be relied upon to supply only genuine items or, in the event that a piece is discovered to be not what it appeared, are prepared to take it back. The auction houses are jealous of their reputation and they too will stand by any description that they give and should it be found to be incorrect will refund the purchase price and take back the item in question.

The modern collector is far more fortunate than his counterpart of the pre-war period because the number of good, reliable reference books now available is considerable, as an examination of the bibliography will show. Before the 1939–45 war there were perhaps half a dozen reliable books – today there are half a dozen reliable ones published every month. This increase in reliable references has led to a great expansion of knowledge with consequent improvements in cataloguing for auctions, museum labelling and in dealers' expertise. The collector can benefit by selected reading and certainly by visits to museums.

Recent technological advances are also of great assistance to the collector in maintaining the collection in prime condition. Modern oils such as WD 40 and certain rust inhibitors have rendered the task of conservation and preservation much simpler. Modern materials and glues have also facilitated restoration, but restoration is a subject of considerable debate and the distinction between restoration and deception can be quite small. The museum approach is that only the minimum amount of necessary restoration is to be undertaken and while it should enhance the appearance or function of the weapon it should still be discernible as restoration when examined closely.

While it is impossible to give any real guidance as to how to spot a fake, some general pointers can be suggested. Look at the metal work, barrel and lock. Is the wear on both reasonably compatible? If not, is there a valid explanation for the differences? Does the furniture, trigger, trigger guard, lock plate, etc., fit snugly into the stock? If at all possible examine the threads of the screws and bolts – on pieces made prior to the mid nineteenth century they were usually hand cut and have a typical appearance. Have any parts been replaced? If so, why? Is the general shape correct? Are there any marks and if so are they appropriate to the piece? Most European countries instituted a system of proof to test the barrels of firearms – if the barrels passed they were stamped; these marks are listed in several reference books. Are they correct for the particular weapon? Many makers signed their weapons, usually on the barrel and lock plate. Is the lettering and text correct for the apparent date of the weapon?

A word of warning must also be given to the collector of antique firearms. They are indeed firearms and as such are subject to certain restrictions and regulations in almost every country in the world. These vary from state to state and country to country and it behoves the collector to inform himself of the local rules and regulations before he begins to collect. In some countries it is sometimes necessary to register antique firearms while in others there is no restriction at all.

PRICE GUIDE

Price lists need to be treated with caution! They can never be more than a generalized guide because there are so many factors which can affect the price of any single piece. The prices quoted in the following list are realistic in the sense that they represent a price paid for that particular piece. However it must be understood that the same piece in different circumstances could realize a very different price. In auction, and most of the prices refer to auction values, the price realized depends entirely on bids received by the house. It may well be that there are several collectors or dealers anxious to acquire a certain piece. Obviously they will bid against one another and so push the price for that particular specimen well above the usual value.

The term market value also needs defining. It can be stated as the generally accepted price for an average example of a particular type; for example the average boxlock, flintlock pocket pistol realizes about £100 to £150. It must be stressed that the figures quoted here are those which might reasonably be expected to be realized at auction. Although the dealers often build their stocks from the auction houses it must be remembered that they are in business to make a profit. If they purchase an item for £120 they will want to sell it for, at the very least, £170–£200 so that the figures quoted do not necessarily represent a buying but rather a selling price through auction. Each and every piece is only worth as much as one person or group is prepared to pay for it and this figure is only really relevant to that particular piece. If a collector or dealer wants a particular piece he will pay for it.

Since this volume is intended to be a useful guide for collectors, a number of pieces well beyond the range of the average collector have been included largely as illustrations of a type.

1. £3,000–£5,000
2, 3. £7,000–£9,000
4. £12,000–£20,000
5. £60,000–£70,000
6. £8,000–£12,000
7. £1,800–£2,500
8. £800–£1,200
9. £6,000–£7,000
10. £1,000–£1,200
11. £1,100–£1,300
12. £4,000–£5,000
13. £2,000–£3,000
14. £1,000–£1,200
15. £7,000–£8,000
16. £12,000–£15,000

17, 18. Not applicable
19. £600–£700
20, 21. £500–£600
22. £500–£700
23. £450–£550
24. £250–£350
25. £500–£600
26. Not applicable
27. £500–£600
28. £500–£600
29. £300–£400
30. £200–£300
31. £350–£450
32, 33, 34. £700–£800
35. £700–£900
36. £200–£300
37. £3,000–£4,000
38. £4,000–£4,500
39. £500–£600
40. £300–£400
41. £1,500–£2,500
42. £700–£900
43. £800–£1,200
44. £1,000–£1,200
45. £1,000–£1,200
46. £150–£200
47. £500–£700
48. £200–£250
49. £350–£450
50. £350–£450
51. £1,200–£1,400
52. £350–£450
53. £300–£400
54. £900–£1,200
55. £350–£450
56. £1,300–£1,500
57. £450–£550
58. £550–£700
59. £500–£700
60. £600–£700
61. £250–£350
62. £200–£300
63. £200–£300
64. £250–£350
65. £800–£1,000
66. £450–£550
67. £1,000–£1,200
68. £10,000–£12,000
69. £1,000–£1,300
70. £1,000–£1,500
71. £600–£700
72. £900–£1,100
73. £700–£1,000
74. £2,000–£2,500
75. £1,200–£1,400
76. £1,200–£1,500
77. £1,500–£1,800
78. £1,800–£2,000
79. £450–£550
80, 81, 82. £1,300–£1,500
83, 84. £4,500–£6,000
85. £800–£1,000
86. £350–£450
87. £350–£450
88. £1,500–£2,000
89. £7,000–£9,000
90. £6,000–£7,000
91. £600–£700
92. £400–£500
93. £5,000–£7,000
94. £3,000–£5,000
95. £1,200–£1,500
96. £600–£700
97. £2,000–£3,000
98. £1,000–£1,200
99. £300–£400
100. £5,000–£6,000
101. £500–£700
102. £350–£450
103. £100–£150
104. £400–£500
105, 106. £1,000–£1,200
107. £6,000–£10,000
108. Not applicable
109. £80–£120
110. £500–£700
111. £200–£400
112. £250–£400
113. £500–£700
114. £800–£1,000
115. £400–£600
116. £1,500–£2,000
117. £1,100–£1,300
118. £400–£500
119. £2,000–£2,500
120. £350–£450
121. £300–£400
122. £300–£400
123. £500–£700
124. £800–£1,000
125. £150–£300
126. £150–£250
127. £150–£250
128. £2,500–£3,500
129. £200–£300
130. £200–£300
131. £200–£250
132. £500–£650
133. £550–£650
134. £400–£500
135. £150–£250
136. £450–£550
137. £200–£300
138. £25,000–£30,000
139. £2,000–£3,500
140, 141, 142. £800–£1,000
143. £2,000–£3,000
144. £600–£700
145. £3,000–£3,500
146. £900–£1,300
147. £700–£800
148. £650–£800
149. £600–£700
150. £800–£900
151. £500–£700
152. £600–£800
153. £600–£800
154, 155. £3,000–£4,500
156. £300–£400
157. £600–£800
158. £700–£900
159. £350–£450
160. £500–£600
161. £200–£300
162. £200–£300
163. £400–£600
164. £700–£800
165. £200–£400
166. £1,750–£2,500
167. £2,000–£2,500
168. £2,500–£3,500
169. £2,500–£3,500
170. £1,000–£1,200
171, 172. £750–£900
173. £300–£400
174. £250–£300
175. £1,500–£2,000
176. £300–£400
177. £300–£500
178. £150–£200
179. £100–£150
180. £100–£150

181. £100–£150
182. £300–£400
183. £200–£300
184. £200–£300
185. £200–£300
186. £150–£250
187. £200–£300
188. £1,100–£1,300
189, 190. £300–£500
191. £500–£600
192. £350–£500
193. £800–£1,000
194. £150–£250
195. £300–£500
196. £300–£500
197. £300–£500
198. £300–£500
199. £300–£500
200. £300–£500
201. £300–£500
202. £300–£500
203. £300–£500

Below: Bullet moulds – most cased sets of pistols or longarms included a bullet mould among the accessories. The one on the right is for a percussion revolver, and casts two bullets – one circular, one conical. Worth anything between £16 and £80 each.

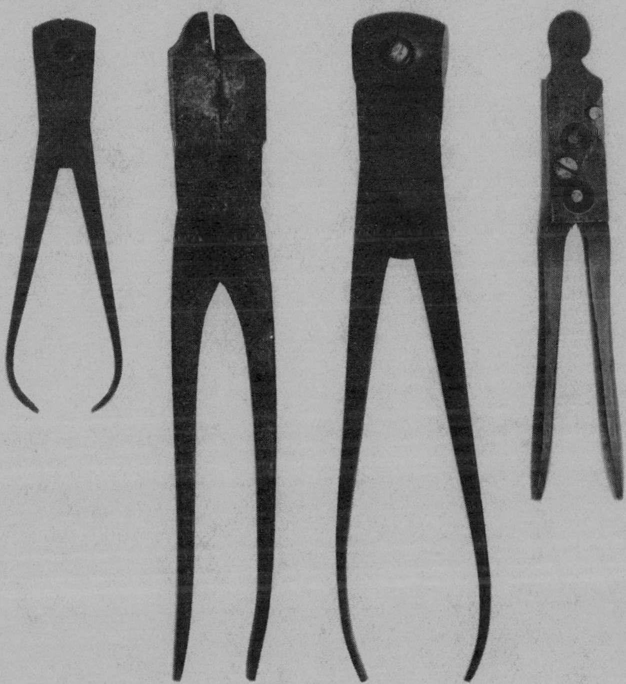

BIBLIOGRAPHY

There are probably more books dealing with firearms than any other type of arms and armour, but this list includes only those which are still reasonably available. There are often relevant articles in such magazines as *The Handgunner*, *Guns Review*, *Guns and Ammo*, and *Target Gun* as well as specialist publications such as the *Journal of the Arms and Armour Society* and the *Journal of the Historical Breechloading Small Arms Association*.

ABRIDGMENTS of the Patent Specification Relating to Firearms, 1588–1855. London, 1960

ALBOROUGH, W. *Confederate Handguns*. Pennsylvania, 1963

ATKINSON, J. *The British Duelling Pistol*. London, 1978

BAILEY D. W., and NIE, D. *English Gunmakers*. London, 1978

BAXTER, D. *Superimposed Load Firearms, 1360–1860*. Hong Kong, 1966

BEDFORD, C. *Early Firearms*. New York, 1969

BLACKMORE, H. L. *British Military Firearms*. London, 1969

BLAIR, C. *Pistols of the World*. London, 1968

— (ed.) *Pollards History of Firearms*. London 1983

BOOTHROYD, G. *Guns and Gun Collecting*. London, 1972

— *The Handgun*. London, 1970

BOUDRIOT, J. *Armes à Feu Françaises Modèles Réglementaires*. Paris, 1961–5

BROOKER, R. E. *British Military Pistols*, 1603–1888. Florida, 1978

BYRON, D. *Gunmarks*. New York, 1979

CAREY, A. M. *English, Irish & Scottish Firearms Makers*. London, 1967

CHAMBERLAIN, W. and TAYLERSON, A. *Adams Revolvers*. London, 1976

DOVE, P. *The Revolver*. 1858. London reprint, 1968

DOWELL, W. C. *The Webley Story*. York, 1962

DUNLAP, J. *American, British & Continental Pepperbox Firearms*. San Francisco, 1967

FORD, G. *A Collection of Pistol Points*. London, N.D.

FROST, H. G. *Blades & Barrels*. Texas, 1972

GAIERT, C. *Four Centuries of Liège Gunmaking*. London, 1976

GARDNER, R. *Small-Arms Makers*. New York, 1953

GEORGE, J. N. *English Pistols and Revolvers*. 1938

GLENDENNING, I. *British Pistols & Guns*. London (reprint), 1967

GLUCKMAN, *United States Martial Pistols & Revolvers*. Harrisburg, 1960

HATCH, A. *Remington Arms*. U.S.A., 1956

HAYWARD, J. F. *The Art of the Gunmaker*. Vol. I. London, 1965; Vol. II. London, 1963
HELD, R. *The Age of Firearms*. Northfield, 1970
HOFF, A. *Dutch Firearms*. London, 1978
HOGG, I. *Illustrated Encyclopedia of Firearms*. London, 1978
JINKS, R. *History of Smith & Wesson*. N. Hollywood, 1977
KENNARD, A. N. *French Pistols & Sporting Guns*. London, 1972
KIST, J. B. and PUYPE, J. P. *Dutch Muskets & Pistols*. London, 1974
LAVIN, J. D. *A History of Spanish Firearms*. London, 1965
LENK, T. *The Flintlock*. London, 1965
LEWES, B. *Small Arms & Ammunition in the U.S. Service, 1776–1865*. Washington, 1968
LINDSAY, M. *One Hundred Great Guns*. London, 1968
LOGAN, H. *Underhammer Guns*. Harrisburg, 1960
LUGS, J. *Firearms Past & Present* (2 Vols). London, 1973
MYATT, *19th Century Firearms*. London, 1979
NEAL, R. J. and JINKS, R. G. *Smith & Wesson, 1857–1945*. London, 1966
NEAL, W. K. and BACK, D. *British Gunmakers, their Trade Cards, Cases & Equipment*. Warminster, 1980
— *Forsyth & Co. Patent Gunmaker*. London, 1969
— *Great British Gunmakers*. London, 1975
— *The Mantons*. London, 1967
— *The Mantons Supplement*. London, 1978
NORTH, A. and HOGG, I. *Guns & Gunsmiths*. London, 1978
PETERSON, H. L. (ed.). *Encyclopaedia of Firearms*. London, 1964
— *The Book of the Gun*. London, 1962
— and ELMAN, R. *The Great Guns*. New York, 1971
— *The Remington Historical Treasury of American Guns*. 1966
ROADS, C. *The Gun*. London, 1978
SUTHERLAND, R. and WILSON, L. *The Book of Colt Firearms*. Kansas City, 1971
TAYLERSON, A. *Revolving Arms*. London, 1967
— *The Revolver, 1865–1888*. London, 1966
— *The Revolver, 1889–1914*. London, 1970
—, and ANDREW, R. FRITH, J. *The Revolver, 1818–65*. London, 1968
WILKINSON, F. *Antique Firearms*. London, 1969
— *Antique Guns & Gun Collecting*. London, 1985
— *British & American Flintlocks*. London, 1971
— *Flintlock Pistols*. London, 1968
— *Illustrated Book of Pistols*. London, 1979
— *The World's Great Guns*. London, 1981
WINANT, L. *Early Percussion Firearms*. London, 1959
— *Firearms Curiosa*. London, 1956

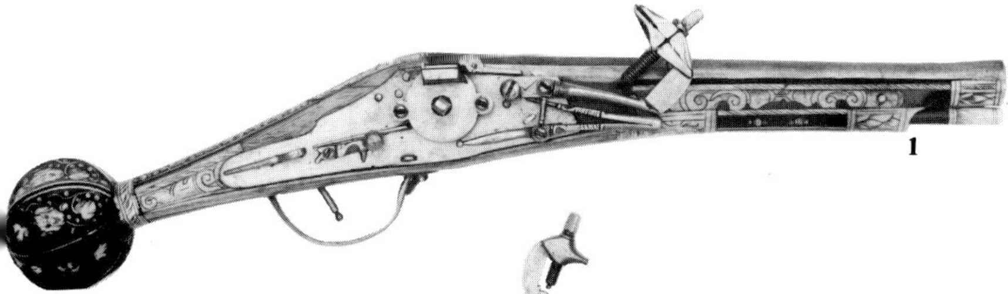

1

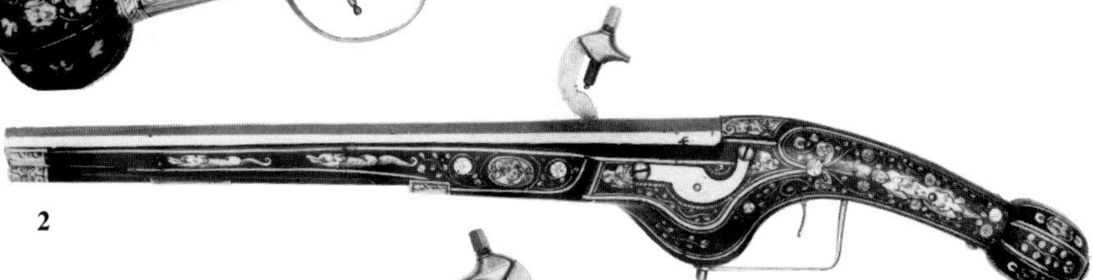

2

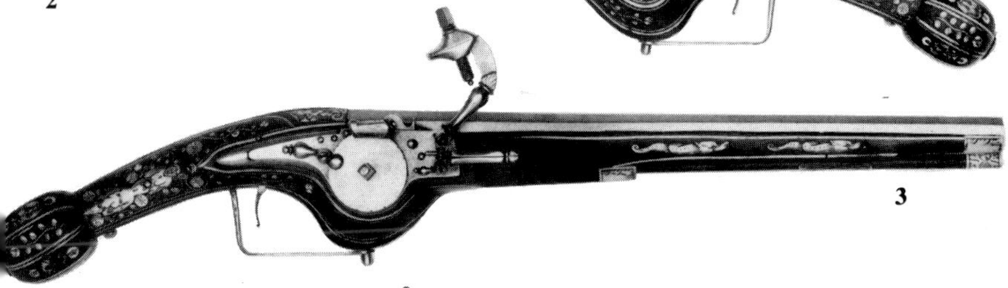

3

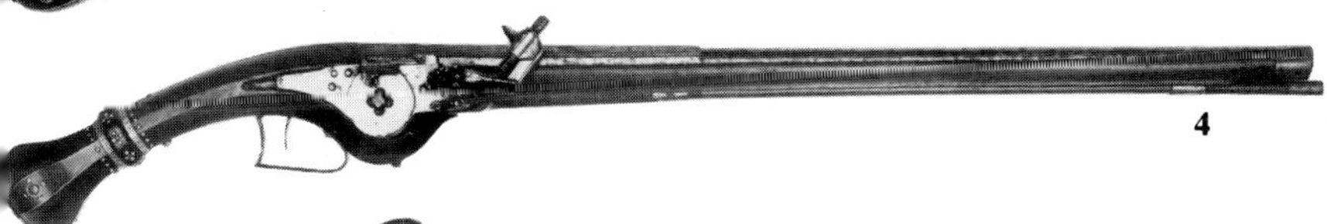

4

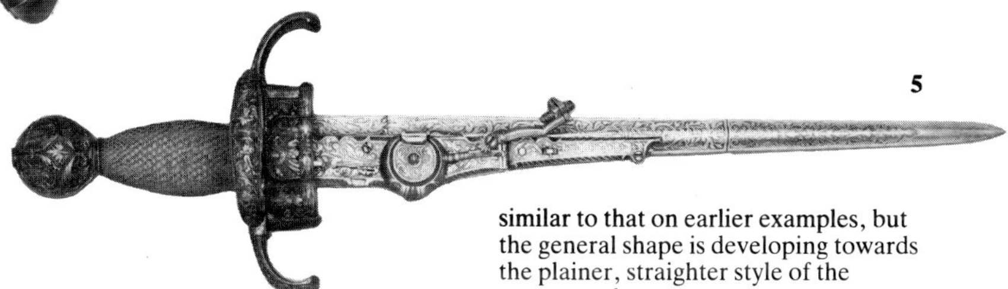

5

1. A fairly typical German wheel-lock pistol of the sixteenth century. The stock, usually of walnut, is inlaid with ivory, sometimes horn, and the large ball butt is common to this type of pistol. The lock plate will often give a rough dating for the weapon: large and with external catches will usually indicate that it is early; the plainer it is the later it is likely to be.

2 and 3. Few specimens will be found as fine as this example of a later French wheel-lock pistol with the plainer lock plate and characteristic deep belly so often found on wheel-locks of the seventeenth century. The decoration is similar to that on earlier examples, but the general shape is developing towards the plainer, straighter style of the seventeenth-century weapon.

4. A superb and elegant French wheel-lock pistol – few collectors can hope to acquire examples such as this. It has the plain lock and characteristic shape of the seventeenth-century military wheel-lock pistol, but this one is far more decorative.

5. In May 1983 the collection of Arms and Armour from Hever Castle was sold at auction by Sotheby's. This was one of the rare and unusual pieces that realized exceptional prices. It is a combination wheel-lock and dagger dating from the mid sixteenth century and combines Italian and German features.

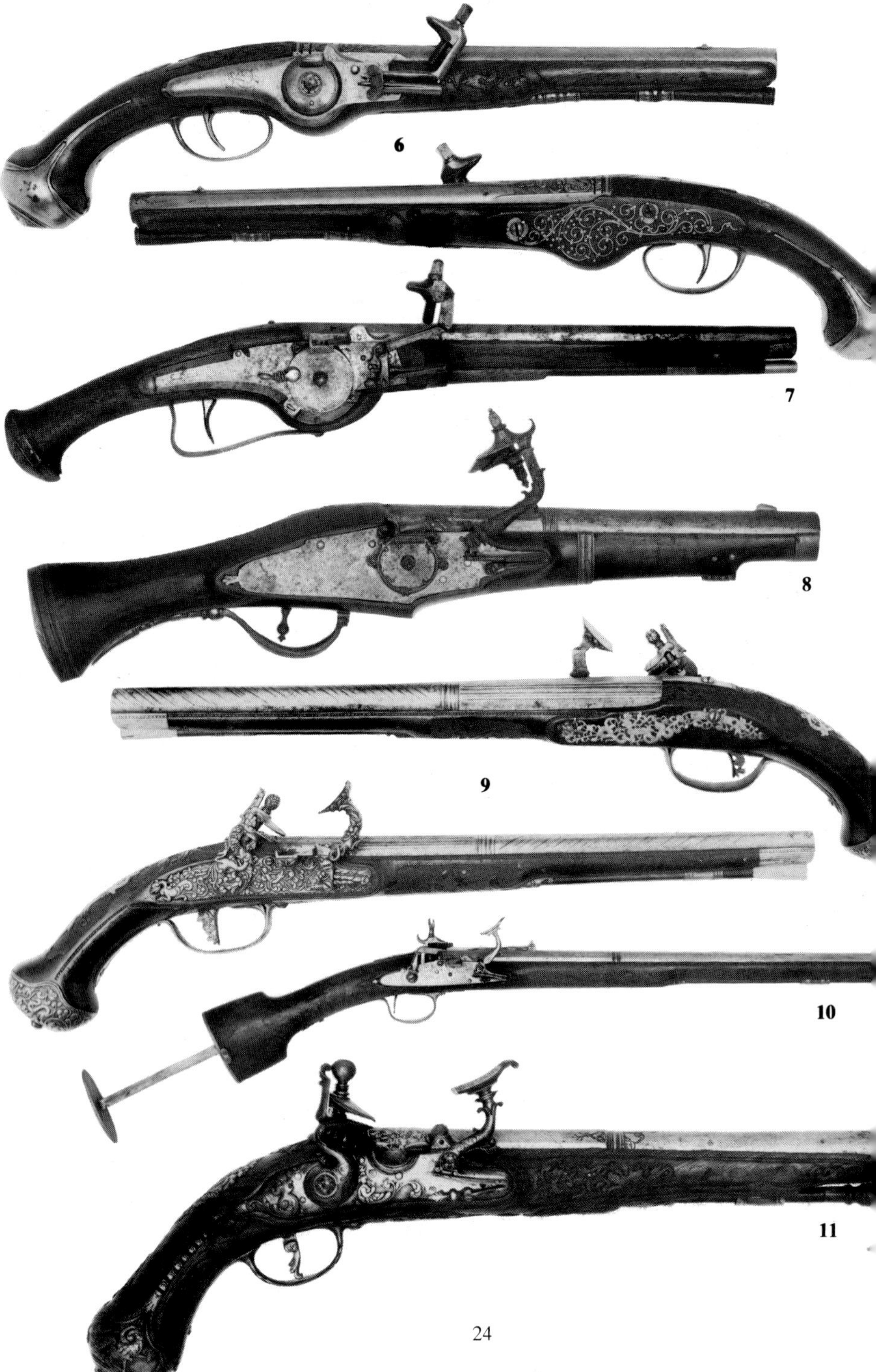

6

7

8

9

10

11

6. A pair of wheel-lock pistols probably made in Thuringia and dating from about 1700. Their stocks are very much like those of the flintlock pistols of the period with the globose pommel and caps and inlaid silver wire decoration. The wheels are covered with brass discs and the breeches are chiselled.

7. Like the majority of military weapons this early seventeenth-century wheel-lock is functional with only a faceted butt cap as decoration. The stock is plain and the lock lacks all non-essential features such as wheel covers, safety catches and decoration.

8. An Italian wheel-lock, probably from Brescia and dating from about 1700. The lock and barrel have been re-stocked and this reduces its value.

9. Brescia in Italy was famous for the skill of its metal-workers and this pair of snaphaunce holster pistols is typical of the fine chiselling done by the gunsmiths. The locks are decorated with high-relief scrolls and mythical creatures. Like the previous pistol these were restored at sometime during the latter part of the eighteenth century although locks and barrels are probably late seventeenth century.

10. A late seventeenth- or early eighteenth-century snaphaunce carbine with an extending butt which consists of a metal arm with an oval end-plate. The extension can be withdrawn from the butt and locked into position so that the weapon could be used as a pistol or as a shoulder arm.

11. Another Brescian snaphaunce pistol, but lacking the elaborate decoration of the earlier example. The pistol is homogeneous, even retaining its original ramrod. The stock has some carved decoration.

12. An early example of the true flintlock pistol with pan cover and steel combined to form the frizzen. The cock has the early feature of being secured from the inside – no screw being visible. Despite its simplicity, traces of worm and lack of ramrod, the rarity of such a piece would ensure a high price.

13. A seventeenth-century flintlock pistol with the early feature of a sear operating through the lock plate to act on the tail of the cock. Fitted just in front of the cock is a buffer intended to prevent the cock swinging too far forward.

12

13

14

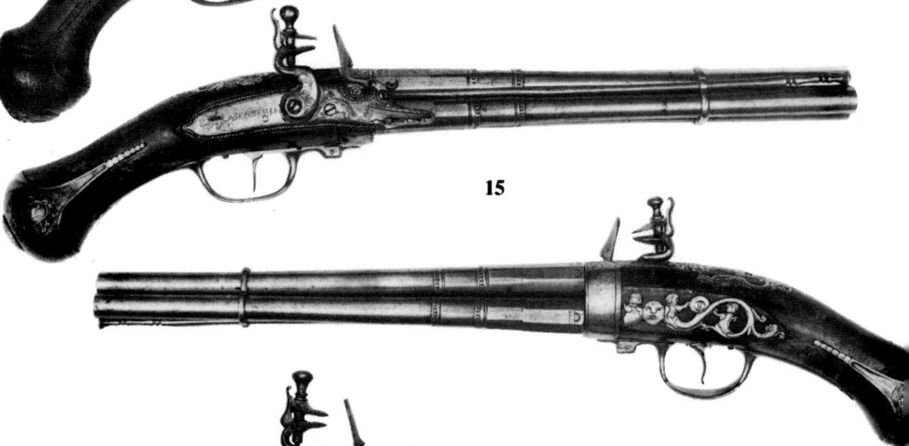

15

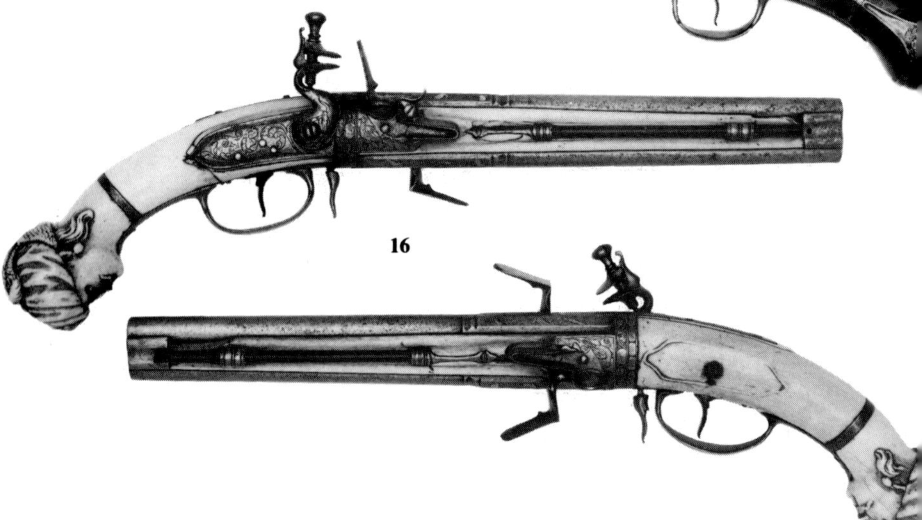

16

14. A Dutch flintlock pistol signed COSTER A UTRECHT, made in about 1680 but restocked in about 1740. The Dutch gunmaking trade flourished during the seventeenth and early eighteenth centuries and pistols with carved ivory stocks were a speciality.

15. A pair of three-barrelled flintlock pistols of the late seventeenth century, probably made in Moravia or Bohemia. The barrels are locked into place by the trigger guard which retracts to allow their movement. The lock plates are signed LA SEPESENBA, an unrecorded maker. The style of barrels and general appearance are typical of pistols of this period.

16. These pistols, made in Maastricht late in the seventeenth century, have ivory butts chiselled into turbanned heads. They have twin barrels, set one above the other, rotated after unlocking them with the catch in front of the trigger guard.

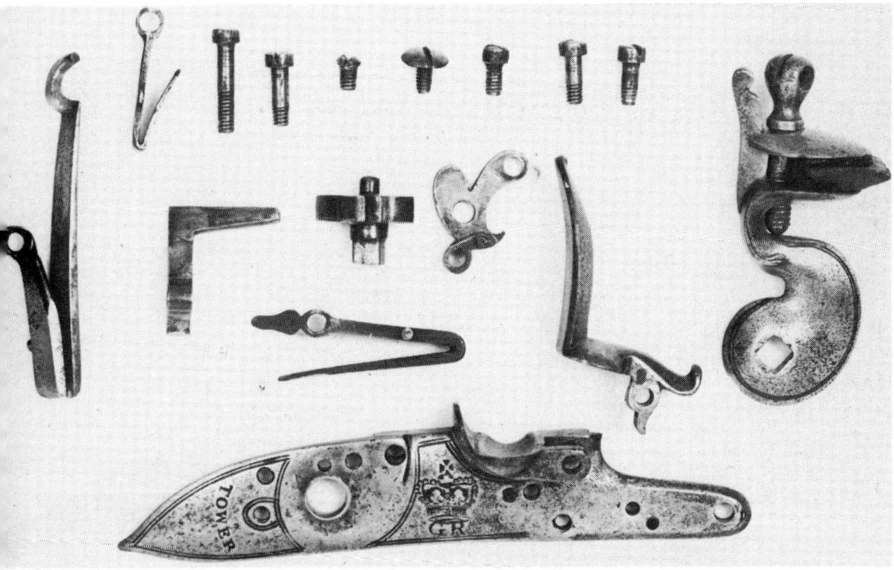

17

17. This dis-assembled flintlock is from a Sea Service pistol of about 1800, but is fairly typical of most locks from the middle of the eighteenth century to about 1820. Later there were various refinements such as small rollers to reduce friction at bearing points.

18. The lock of a Heavy Dragoon flintlock pistol made by F. Jordan. The crowned G.R. indicates that the weapon was official issue as does the word TOWER. Unfortunately for collectors the practice of dating locks ended in 1764.

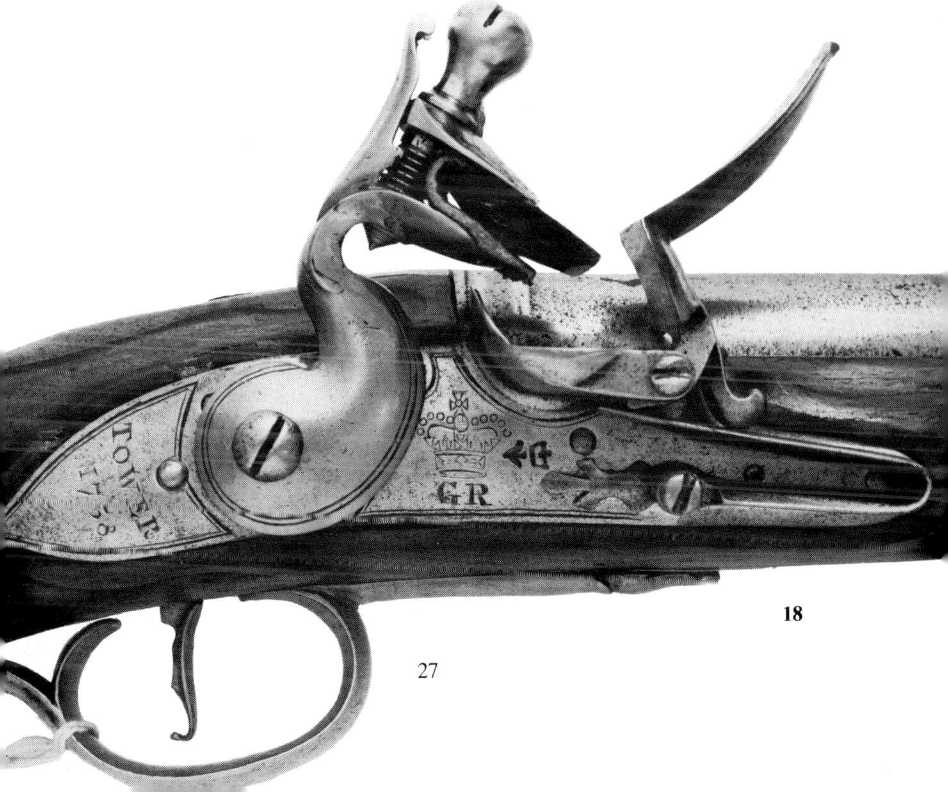

18

19. A good Sea Service flintlock pistol, the lock signed WILLIS and dated 1758. The furniture is brass of regulation style and the whole is in generally good condition, but the value would be somewhat reduced because the cock is not original although apparently of some age.

20 and 21. An early nineteenth-century French trooper's flintlock pistol of the AN XIII type. The lock, like many French military ones, has an iron plate and a brass pan. It later found its way to Ireland for the barrel bears a census number such as was stamped on all pistols in that country in 1843.

22. In 1799 Simon North was awarded a contract to supply military flintlocks and this is one of these weapons. Many of the early American pistols were strongly influenced by French design and this pistol is very similar to the French Model 1777. (Private Collection)

23. British Sea Service flintlock pistol of about 1800 with 12-inch barrel, full stock, brass fittings and a side belt hook. Many such pistols will be found to have a date stamped into the stock.

24. The lion crest on the lock plate of this pistol indicates that the pistol was made for the Honourable East India Company. Unlike the Ordnance, the Company continued to date their locks and this one is dated 1810.

25. Another US official pistol, the Navy Contract weapon of 1808, also supplied by Simon North. Like so many pistols intended for use by naval forces, this model has a belt hook. (Private Collection)

26. Two Sea Service flintlock pistols – one dates from about 1800 and the other is modern. Note the slight difference in the shape of the butts, the triggers and ramrods and the carving around the locks and the cocks. Other indications are the colour of the brass and an abundance of marks which are not found on the original – all these features indicate that the top pistol is a modern copy.

19

20

21

22

23

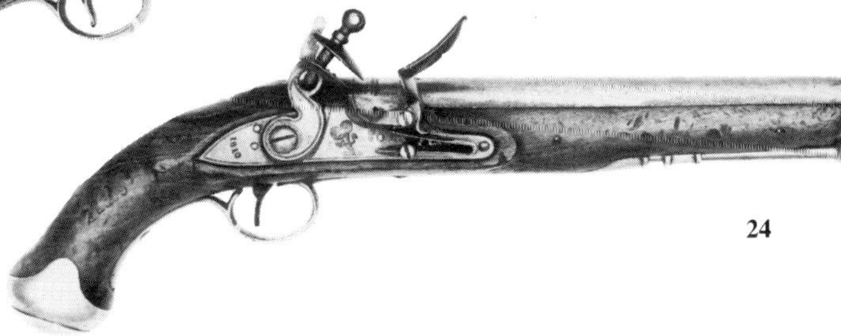
24

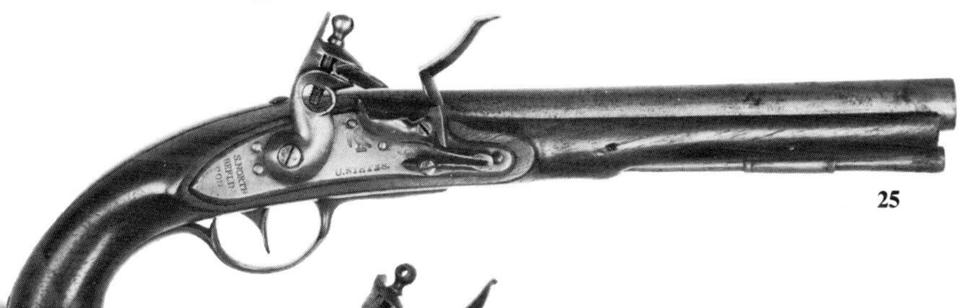
25

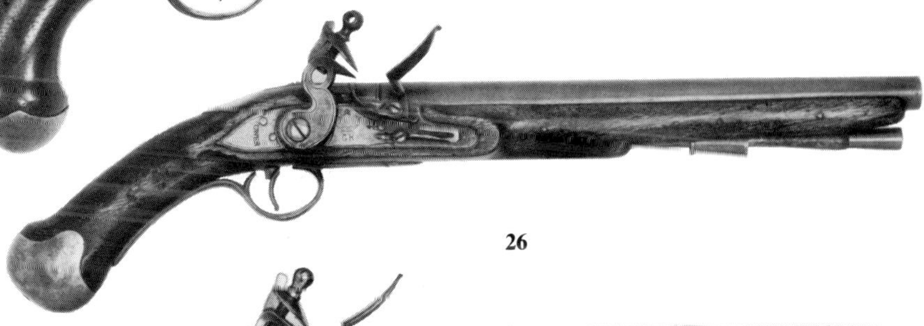
26

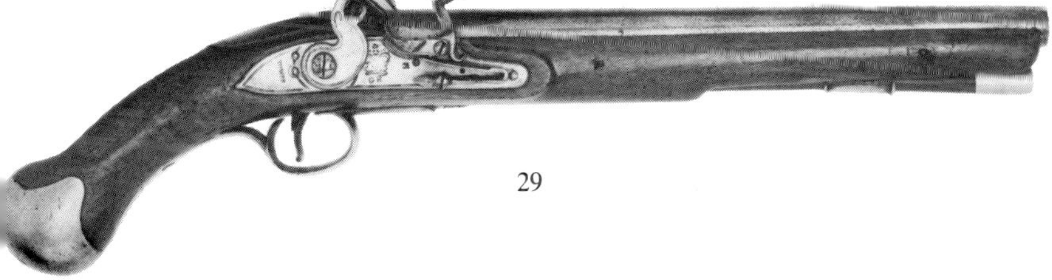

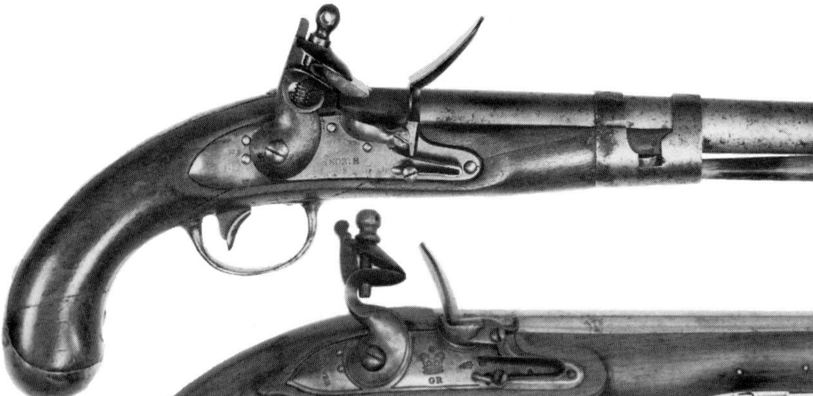

27

28

29

30

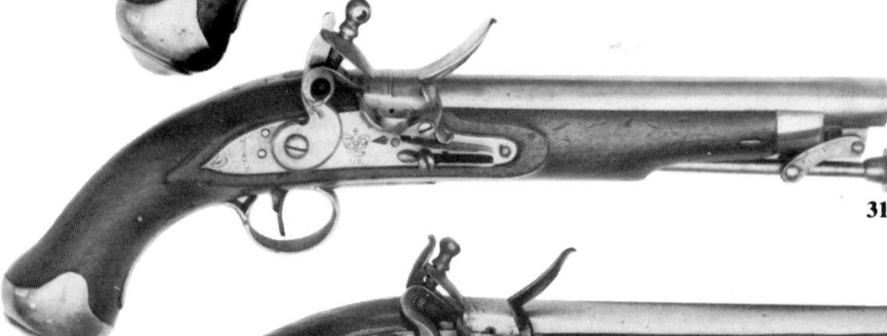

31

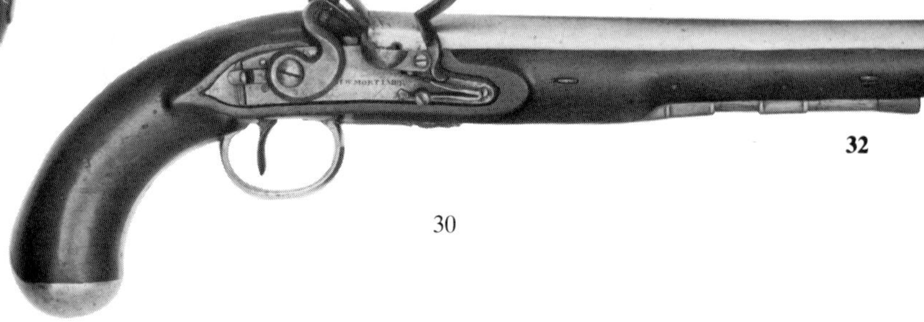

32

27. US Martial pistol of Model 1813 type. Just over 1,100 of these pistols were delivered and only 1,500 were made. The muzzle band is held in place by a spring clip – a feature not adopted on British weapons until the mid nineteenth century. (Private Collection)

28. Trooper's flintlock pistol with 9-inch barrel, the lock with crowned G.R. and inscribed TOWER. It has regulation brass furniture and the trigger guard has the remains of an inscription which could well have been a regimental marking. The pistol is a Modified 1796 Pattern.

33

29. Light Dragoon flintlock pistol with iron ramrod instead of the more usual wooden one. The lock is signed RYAN & WATSON.

30. An H.E.I.C. trooper's pistol, the lock dated 1813. It differs from 24 in having a swivel ramrod – a device intended to reduce the chances of accidental loss.

31. A New Land Pattern pistol of about 1800, also fitted with a swivel ramrod and very similar to but of slightly better quality than the H.E.I.C. pistol.

32 to 34. In 1784 regular deliveries by mail coaches were started in Britain and each coach carried a guard armed with a brace of pistols and a blunderbuss. This pistol is a typical example with its brass barrel, the muzzle of which is stamped FOR HIS MAJESTIES (sic) MAIL COACHES, and the top numbered 88. H. W. Mortimer was responsible for the majority of the flintlock pistols produced for the Post Office.

35. A Belgian trooper's flintlock holster pistol of about 1730. Like most military pistols it is a simple, robust weapon with early features such as the backward curling tip to the trigger and slightly banana-shaped lock. This specimen has been damaged and repaired so that its value is lower than for one in better condition.

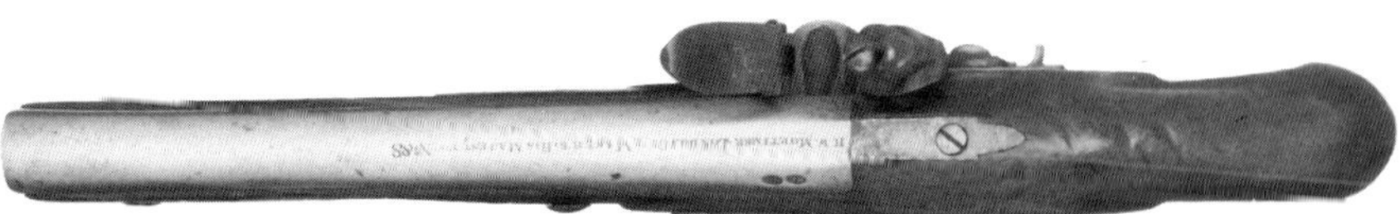

34

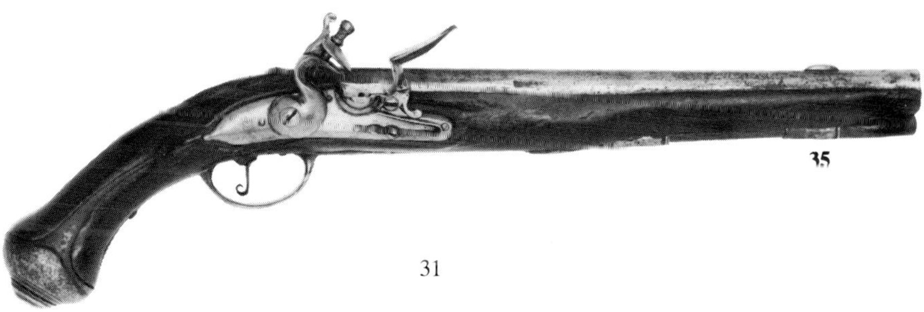

35

36

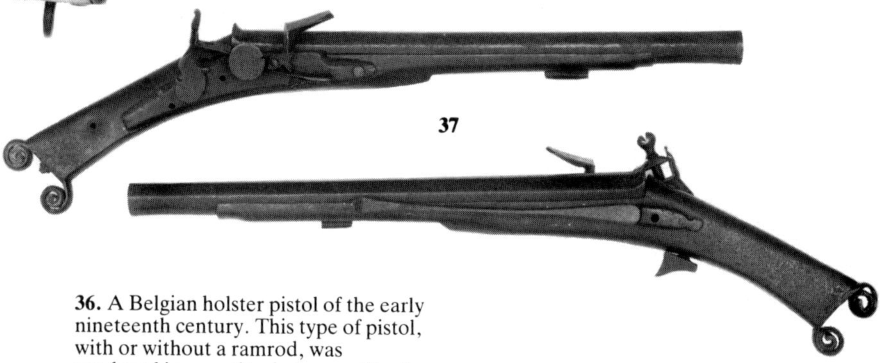

37

36. A Belgian holster pistol of the early nineteenth century. This type of pistol, with or without a ramrod, was produced in quantity, being used by the Belgians as a Sea Service pistol and as a trooper's pistol by the Honourable East India Company.

37. These early Scottish, all-metal pistols are not in very good condition but they are nevertheless of great interest. One is dated 1649 on the pan cover making it probably the earliest dated example of a ramshorn pistol. The stocks are all-metal and although the pistols are very similar they are not a true pair for they differ in detail.

38. This fine, all-metal Scottish pistol is typical of most eighteenth-century examples, with its ramshorn butt, ball trigger and pricker. It is particularly desirable because the butt is set with oval cartouches engraved with the arms of Ross of Kindeace. Any positive association or interesting provenance increases the value of any weapon.

39. Another Scottish dress pistol, a flintlock of about 1820, signed MURDOCK, with waterproof pan, and roller bearing on the frizzen spring. It is complete with ramrod, pricker and ball trigger.

40. A Royal Highland Regiment official Scottish flintlock pistol. This type was issued to Scottish regiments in the late eighteenth century and is simple and robust.

41. Late eighteenth-century Scottish pistols signed T. MURDOCH and fashioned with brass barrels, lock plates, lobed butts and belt hooks. They are inscribed ROBERT KING – presumably a previous owner's name. Although late in period, the all-brass construction makes them rare and consequently desirable.

42. A flintlock typical of the type known as Queen Anne pistols, although it dates from 1765, long after the time of Anne. The barrel is of brass and the frame is signed BRANDER LONDON; the walnut butt has silver mounts and the value is slightly reduced as the cock is not the original.

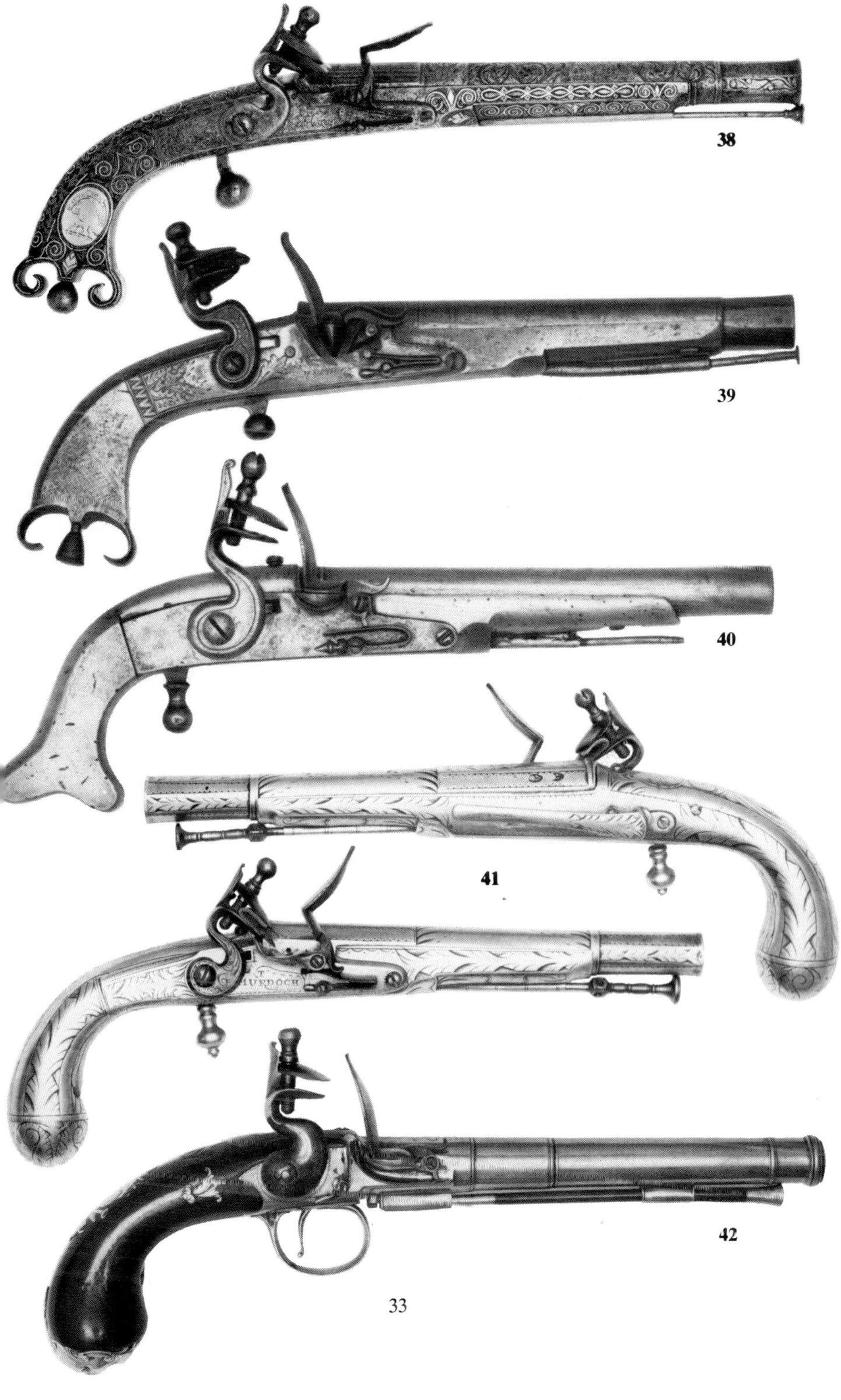

38

39

40

41

42

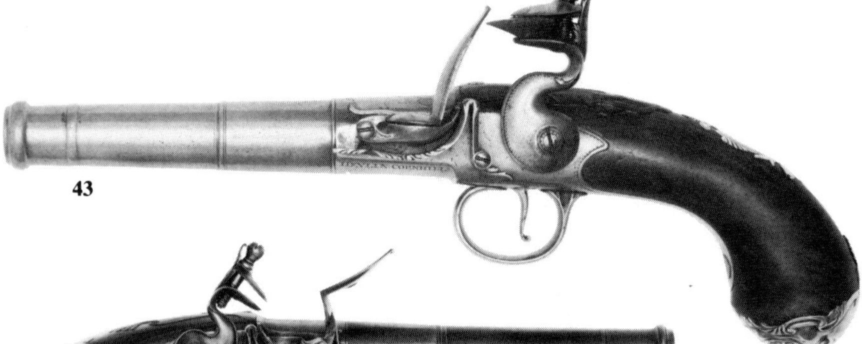

43

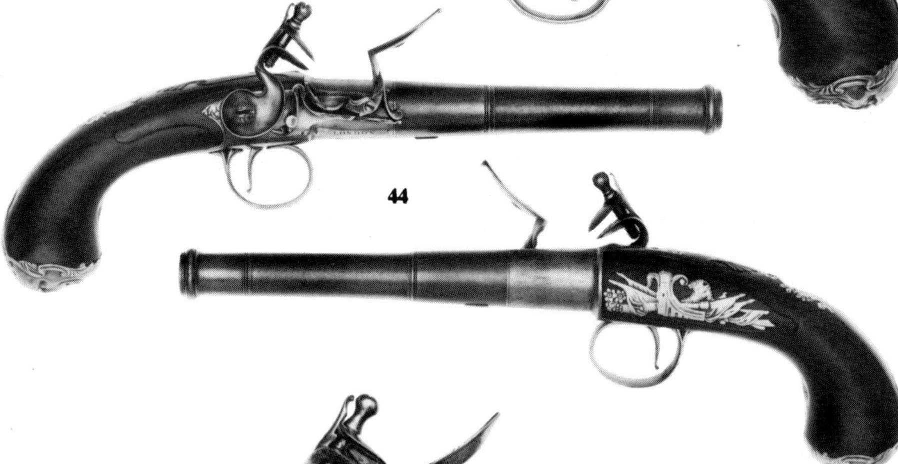

44

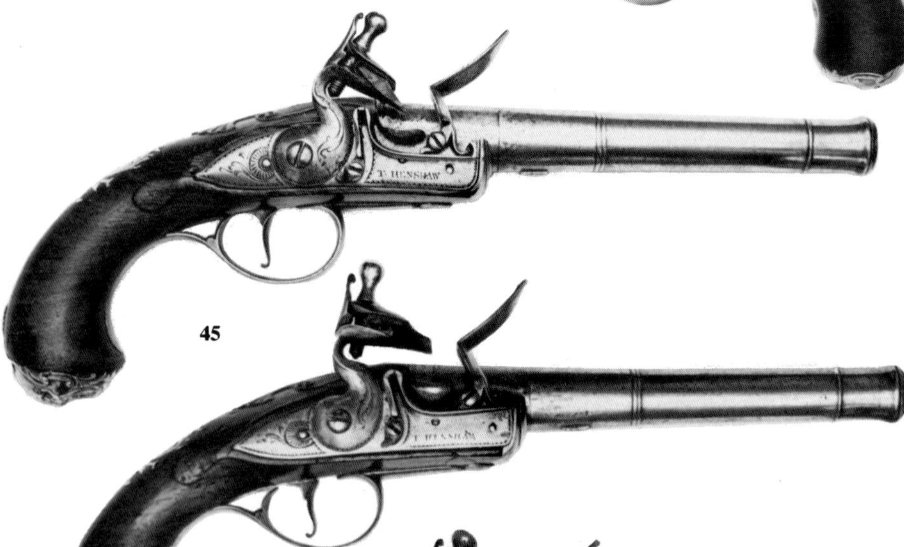

45

46

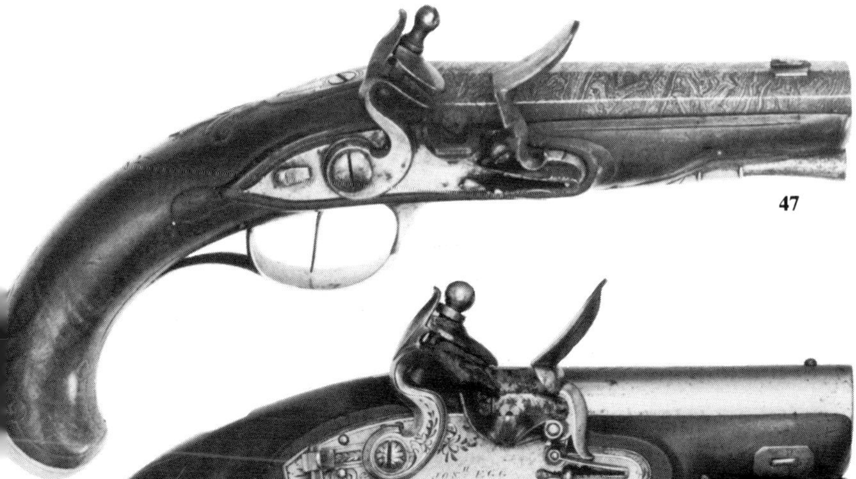

47

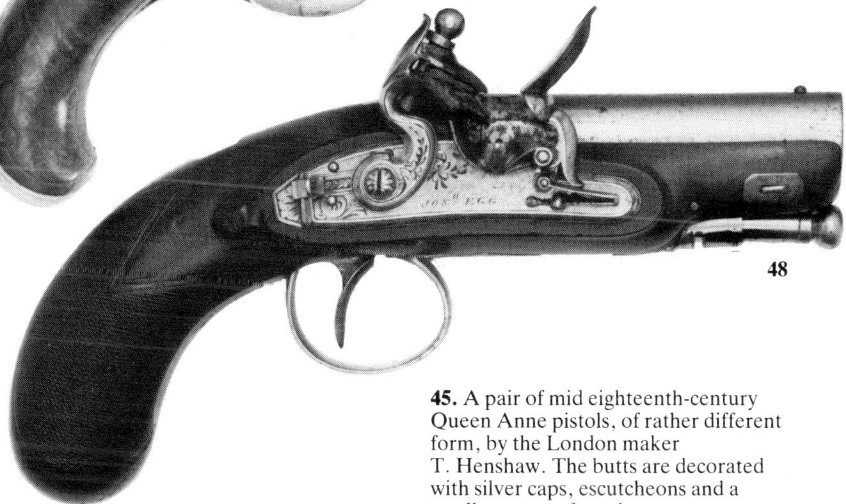

48

43. Another Queen Anne flintlock pistol, of about 1770, but unusual in having the lock mounted on the left side of the stock. The lower side of the frame is signed HEYLIN CORNHILL (London) and the butt has silver mounts typical of the period. The barrel could be unscrewed allowing powder and ball to be placed in the chamber so dispensing with the need of a ramrod.

44. A pair of silver-mounted, Queen Anne flintlock pistols by W. Turvey of London, circa 1740. They have features typical of this type of pistol; upswept frizzen spring, swan-neck cocks and turn-off cannon barrels. The walnut butts are inlaid with military trophies, escutcheon plates and grotesque butt caps.

45. A pair of mid eighteenth-century Queen Anne pistols, of rather different form, by the London maker T. Henshaw. The butts are decorated with silver caps, escutcheons and a small amount of carving.

46. A boxlock flintlock pistol of the late eighteenth century with typical cannon barrel which could be unscrewed for reloading. It has a ring-neck cock and an internal safety catch operated by the trigger guard.

47. An eighteenth-century German flintlock travelling pistol with finely patterned octagonal Damascus barrel. The plain lock is fitted with a push-on safety catch and the rather hooked butt has silver decoration.

48. A flintlock pocket pistol by one of London's best makers, Joseph Egg. The short circular barrel has a gold line at the breech and is inscribed LONDON. The stepped lock, engraved and signed JOS^{H} EGG, is fitted with a waterproof pan and a roller bearing to the frizzen spring. Although attractive, the value is somewhat reduced because the metal has been polished bright.

49. A pair of late eighteenth-century boxlock pocket pistols, signed LONDON. They both have identical slab-sided butts without decoration, and push-on safety catches mounted behind the locks. Pairs usually realize more than just twice the price of one pistol.

50. A slightly more decorative pair of flintlock, boxlock pocket pistols of the late eighteenth century. They are signed EDGE and the rounded butts have the silver wire inlay often found on pistols of this period.

51. A particularly fine over-and-under flintlock pocket pistol with all the refinements of the best quality weapons. The browned barrels have platinum vents and gold poinçons with the maker's name TATHAM & EGG. The locks are similarly signed and are fitted with push-on safety catches. The butt has silver furniture which has the maker's mark of MOSES BRENT. Circa 1820.

52. This may look like an ordinary flintlock pistol, but it is, in fact, a tap-action boxlock pistol. It has two barrels mounted side by side and the pan is fitted with a barrel-like device which enables it to hold two charges of priming powder. By turning this tap each barrel can be fired in turn. The pistol is by Calvert of Leeds and has Birmingham proved barrels. There is a sliding safety catch on the top of the frame which can lock both cock and frizzen.

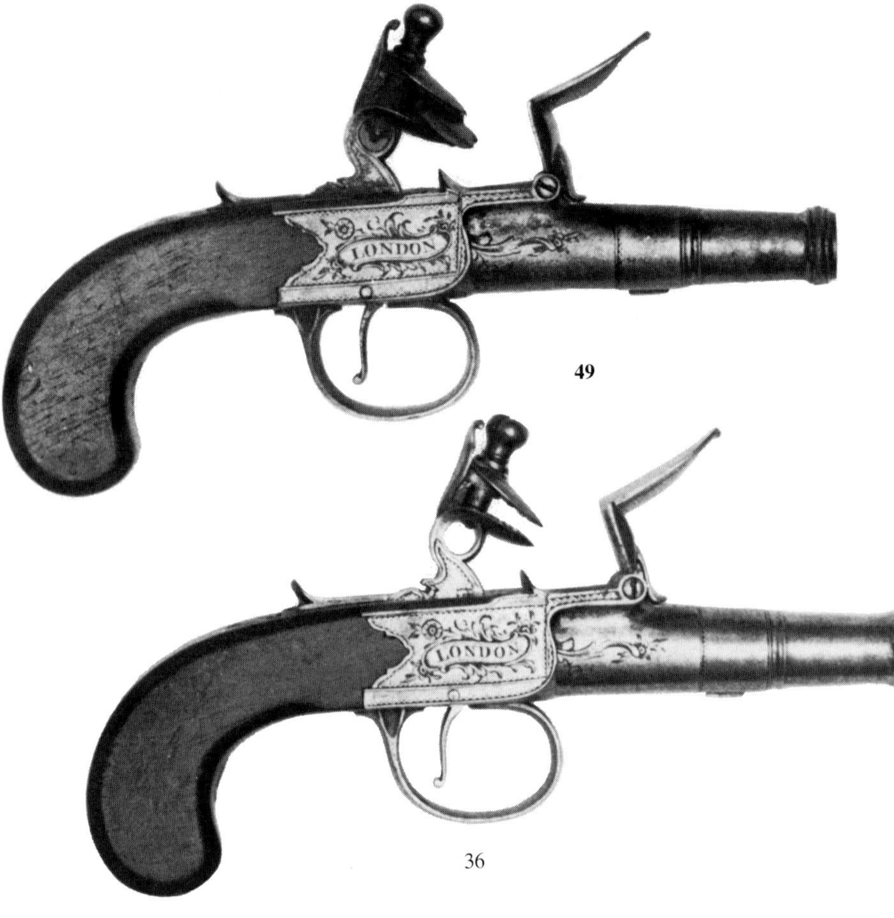

49

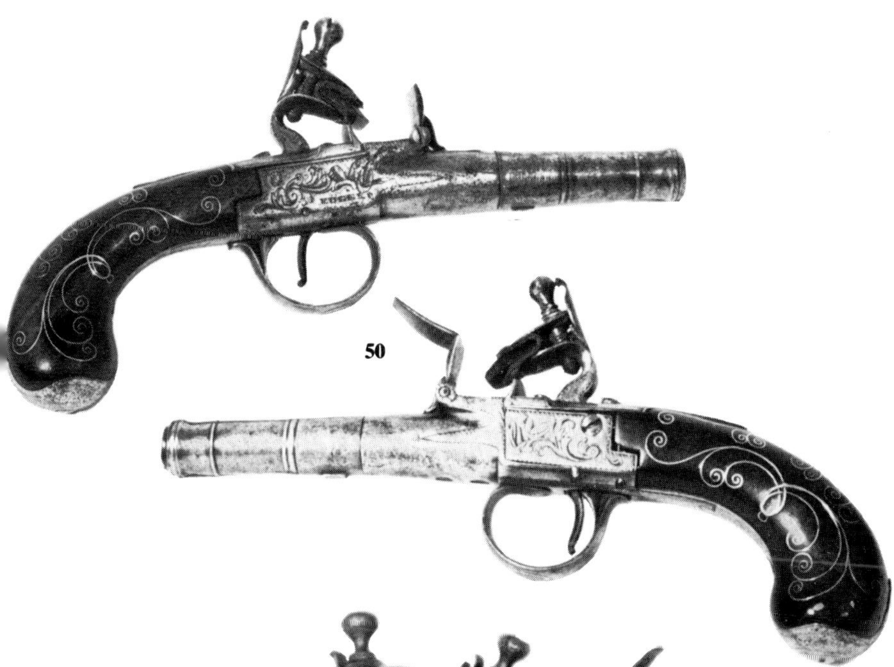

50

51

52

53

54

55

56

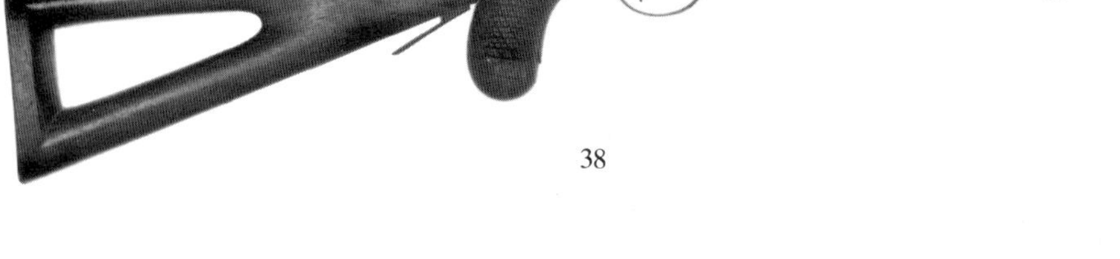

57

53. A Spanish Miquelet lock pistol dating from the first part of the eighteenth century. It has the characteristic ball butt, spurred trigger guard and square jaws of the cock found on the great majority of such pistols. Many were made in the area of Ripoll in northern Spain. The muzzle band and furniture are of decorated brass as on most of these pistols.

54. Made in Ripoll, northern Spain, early in the eighteenth century, this pistol exhibits many features typical of these weapons. The ball butt, Miquelet lock, brass inlay and spurred trigger guard are commonly found on many Spanish pistols. A particularly fine example such as this would be expensive.

55. A silver-mounted, French flintlock holster pistol, the lock signed POITEVIN LAN [?] ANGOULEME, eighteenth century. The pistol has suffered some damage; the side plate and part of the butt cap are lacking, so that its value is reduced.

56. Blunderbuss pistols are popular with collectors and this particularly good example of the late eighteenth century would command a high price. It is in good condition and by a good maker – H. Mortimer of London.

57. Some pistols were so made that a stock could be fitted to the butt thus allowing the weapon to serve as a carbine. This one by Tatham and Egg dates from about 1810.

58. A good Queen Anne boxlock, flintlock pistol, circa 1780. The frame is signed E. NORTH ROYAL EXCHANGE and the butt has inlaid silver wire and a grotesque butt cap.

59. A fairly typical Caucasian or Cossack pistol of the nineteenth century. The ball pommel on the butt is fairly common as are the barrel bands. Niello silver decoration is quite commonly found on these pistols.

60. Another Caucasian Miquelet pistol of the early nineteenth century, with some gold and silver decoration.

58

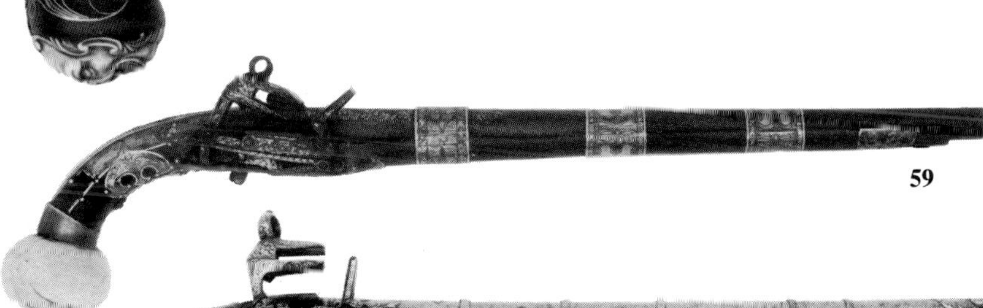

59

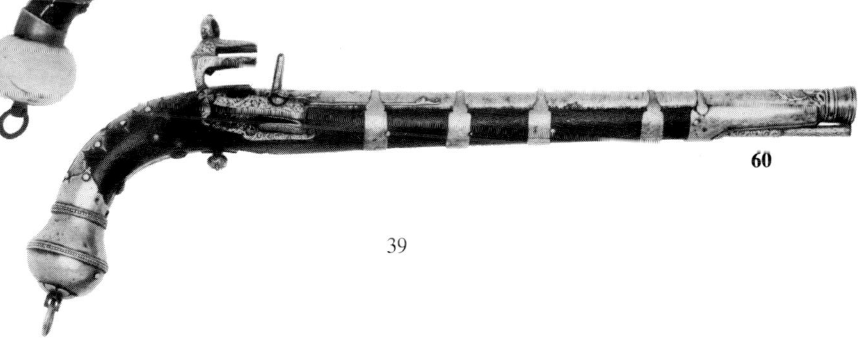

60

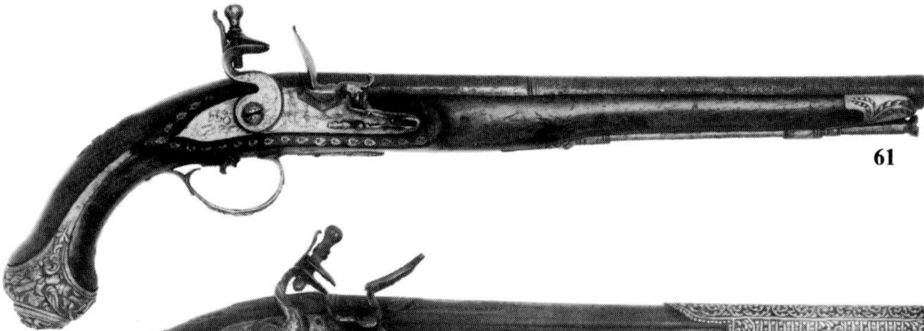

61

62

63

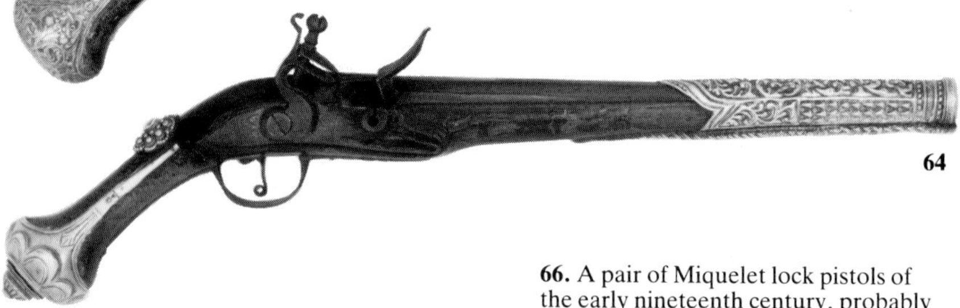

64

61. An early nineteenth-century flintlock, probably from the Balkans for it has some Turkish features as well as standard European details.

62. A nineteenth-century Turkish pistol with characteristic white metal muzzle band and simulated ramrod.

63. A Turkish flintlock pistol of the early nineteenth century, of mediocre workmanship.

64. A slightly more decorative Turkish pistol with some extra decoration in the form of a coral cluster.

65. A very fine pair of nineteenth-century Balkan flintlock pistols with all-metal stocks embossed overall with scrolling foliage, onion-shaped pommels and simulated ramrods.

66. A pair of Miquelet lock pistols of the early nineteenth century, probably from the Balkans. The barrels are engraved and chiselled and the all-metal stocks are decorated overall with bead and foliate patterns.

67. North African or Algerian flintlock pistol of the eighteenth century, decorated with the characteristic panels of coral with silver bands and furniture. The quality is very good and it could well have been intended as a gift such as those sent to the King of England by the Bey of Algiers.

68. An extremely rare pair of breech-loading, silver-mounted pistols, circa 1740, signed CLARKSON LONDINI. The trigger guard is fitted to the breechblock with a coarse thread and as the guard is turned the block is lowered allowing powder and ball to be loaded directly into the breech.

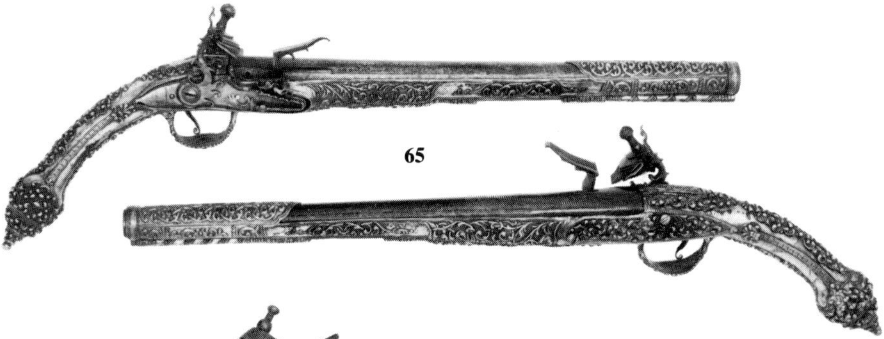

65

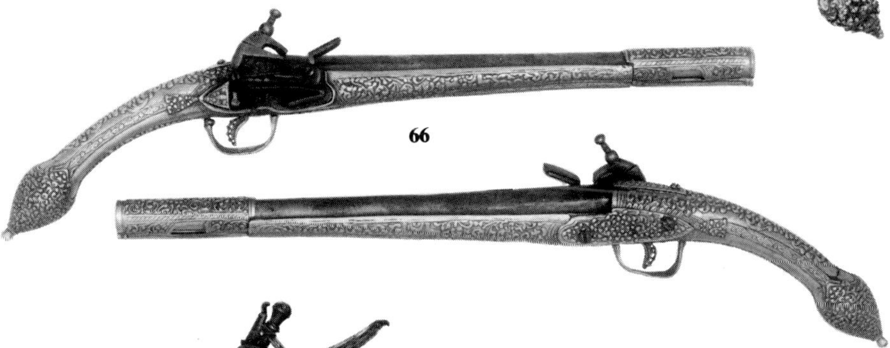

66

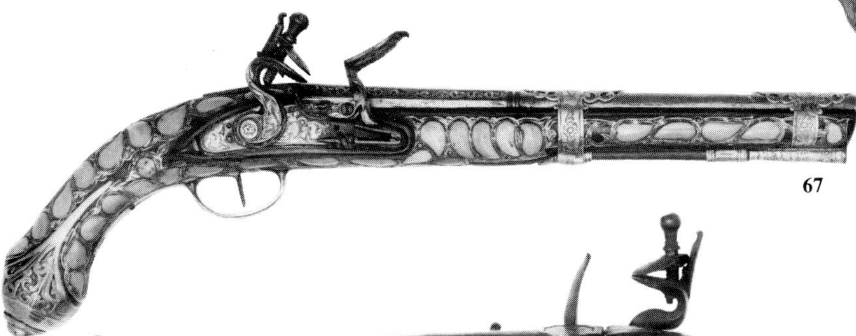

67

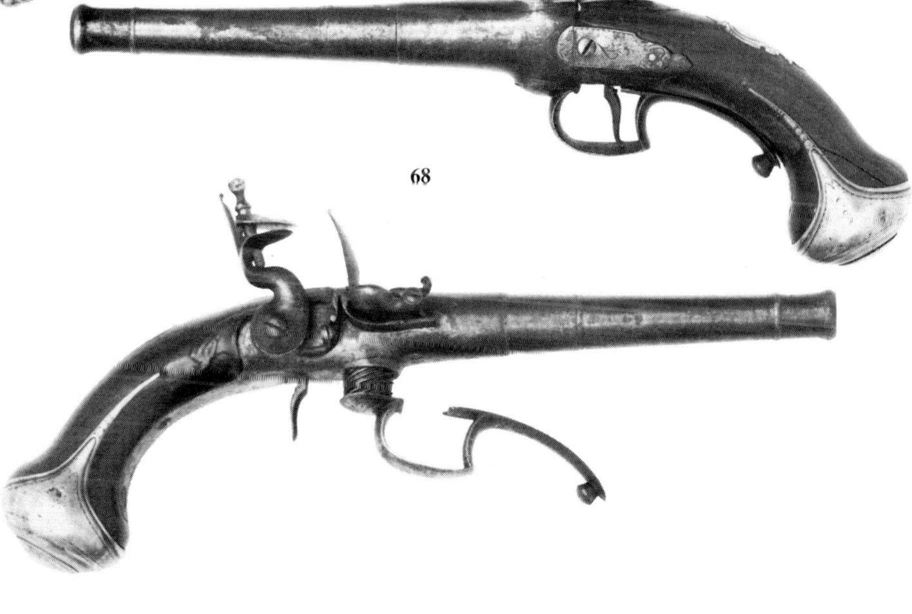

68

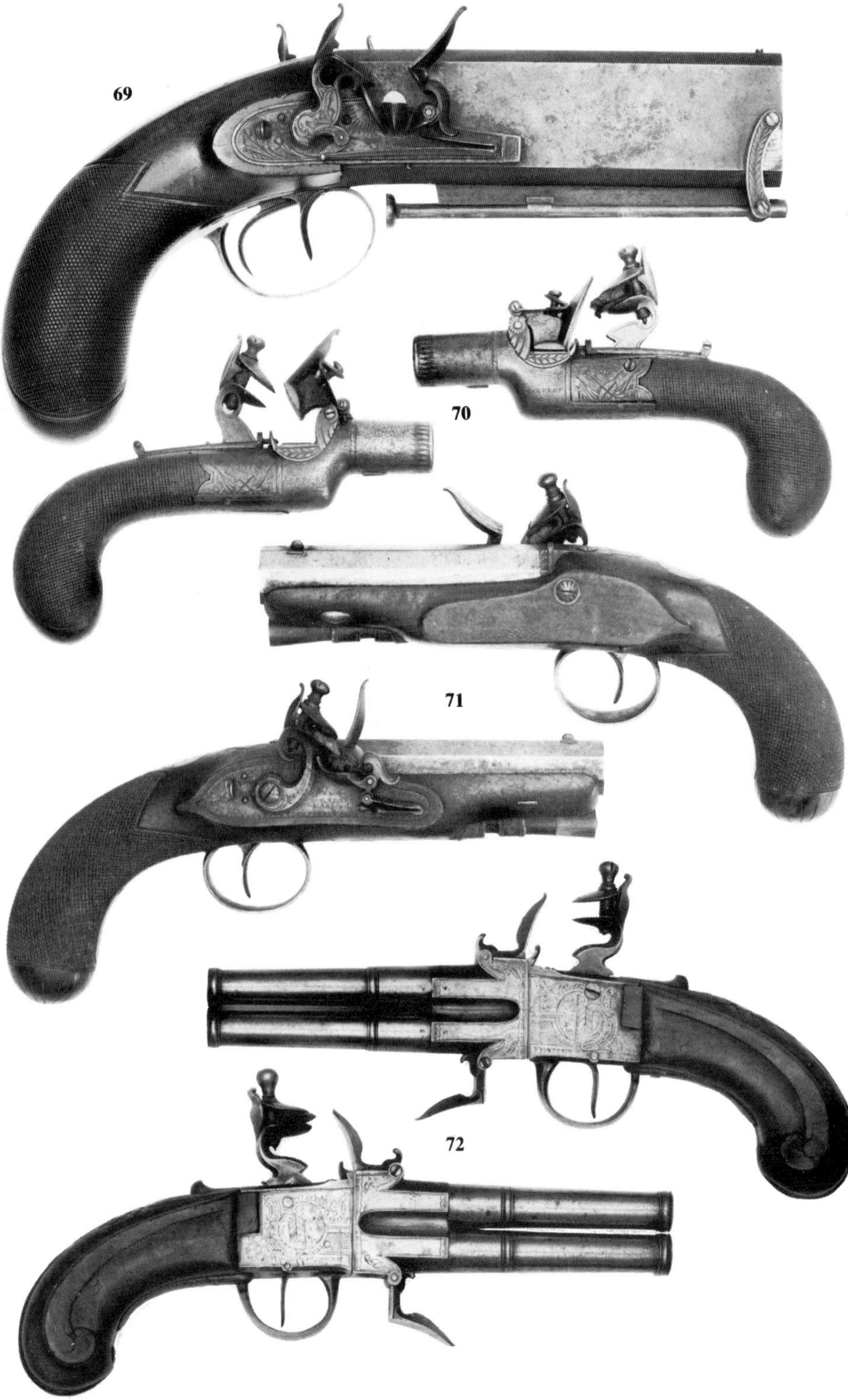

69

70

71

72

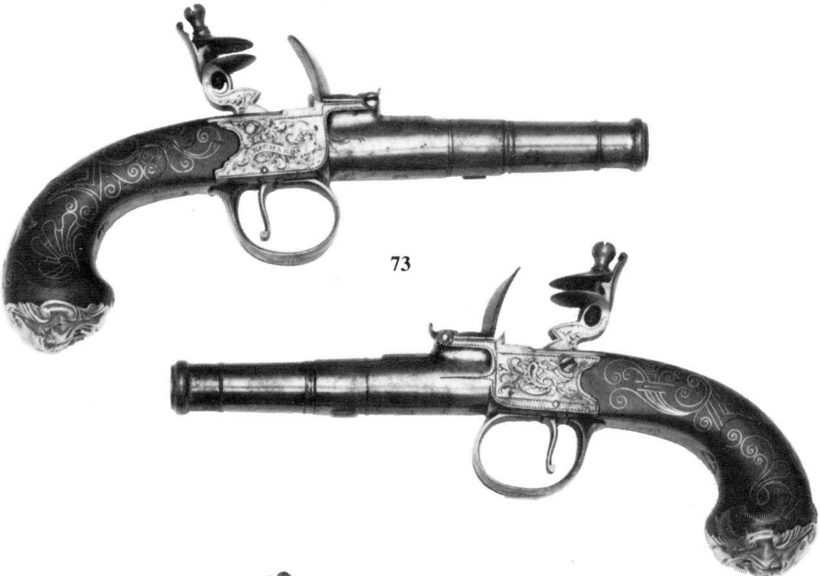

73

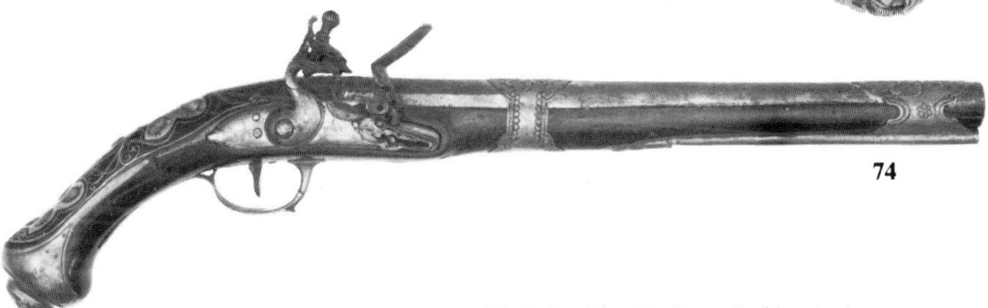

74

69. Unusual over-and-under barrel, flintlock pistol, circa 1825, by W. Jackson of London, with the barrels drilled from a single block of metal. The pistol exhibits all the latest features such as platinum vents and roller bearings. The unusual nature of the weapon would certainly attract interest and this would result in a high price.

70. An unusual pair of flintlock boxlock pocket pistols by Calvert of Leeds, early nineteenth century. The frizzens or steels are fitted to the breech in an uncommon fashion and the round frames are engraved with trophies.

71. Pair of pocket pistols by H. W. Mortimer, early nineteenth century – good average items.

72. Pair of double-barrelled boxlock pocket pistols; the barrel block is rotated to bring the unfired one into the firing position on top. Although Flemish, circa 1770, they are inscribed LONDRE.

73. Pair of silver decorated flintlock, boxlock, overcoat pistols, with London proof and signed RICHARDS. The silver butt caps carry the stamp of Charles Freeth of Birmingham and hallmarks for 1780.

74. Many European gunmakers made pistols for export to the Middle East and Turkey and these were generally far more decorated than the equivalent home market weapon. This is one of a pair, made in Italy for the Turkish market, with chiselled barrels inscribed FORTE FD. SO MUTTI while the locks are signed F. MORETTI. The butts are inlaid with scrolling silver wire and panels set with coral.

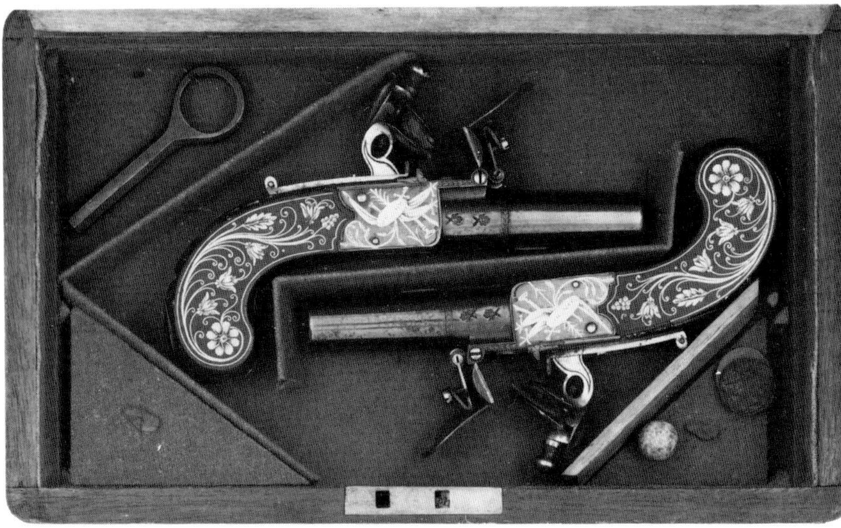

75

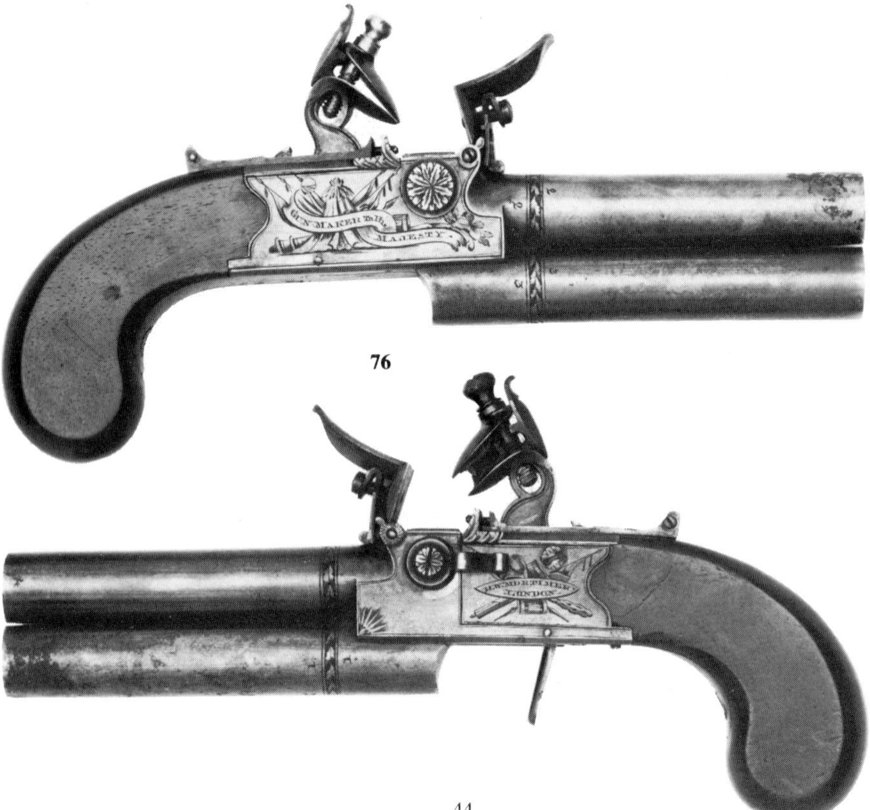

76

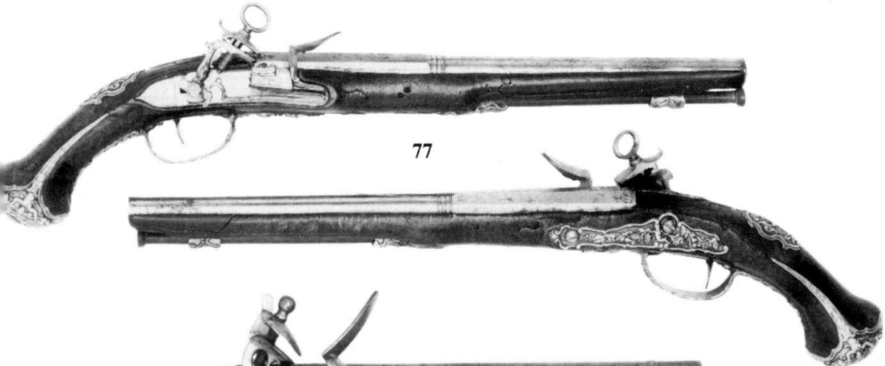

77

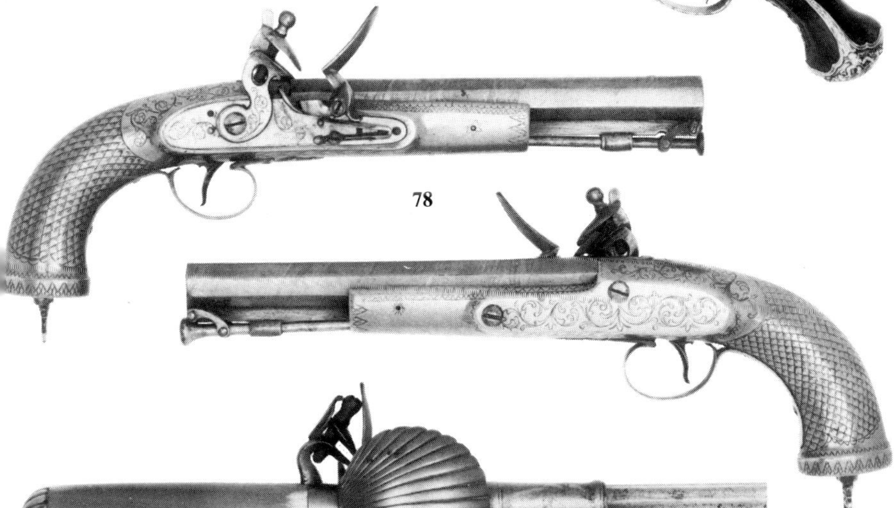

78

79

75. Fine cased pair of elaborately silver-mounted boxlock flintlock pocket pistols with top sliding safety catches with pins to engage and lock the frizzen. The breeches carry private proof marks, circa 1800. These pistols were traditionally the property of Picton, a British Commander at Waterloo.

76. Another pair of pistols by H. & W. Mortimer, this time tap-action flintlock pistols of the late eighteenth century. Top sliding safety catches with pins to secure frizzen.

77. A good pair of early eighteenth-century Miquelet lock Spanish pistols with chiselled barrels and locks and brass furniture.

78. Rare Russian flintlock holster pistols signed KALISNIKOV PSKOW 1801, brass half stocks engraved overall with scrolling foliage, the butts with diamond pattern.

79. A combined flintlock pistol and sword of the late eighteenth century. Although combination weapons usually emphasize the worst features of both components they are not common and are very collectable.

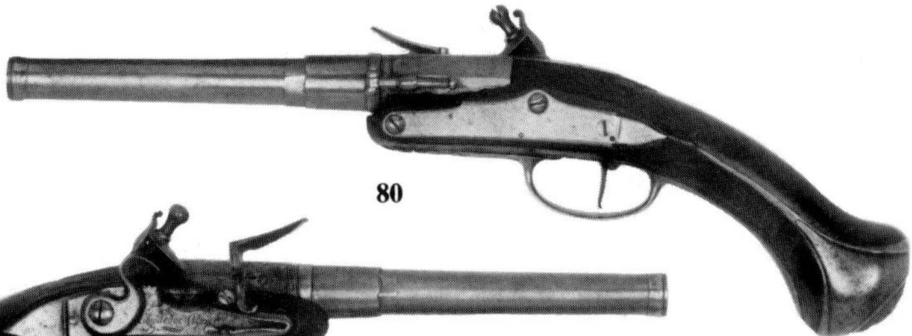

80

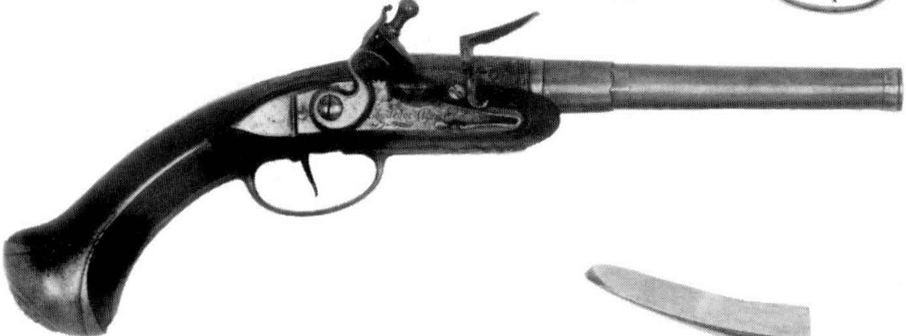

81

82

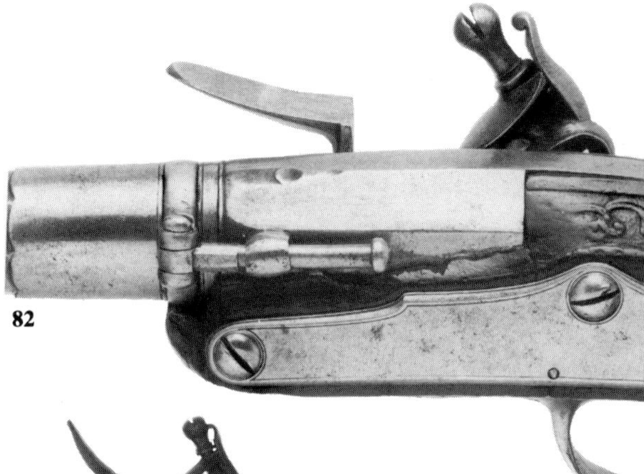

83

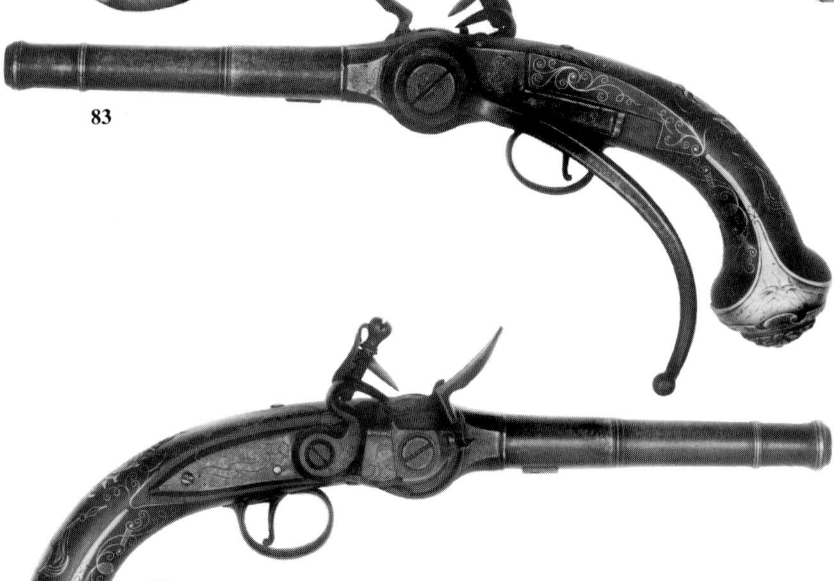

84

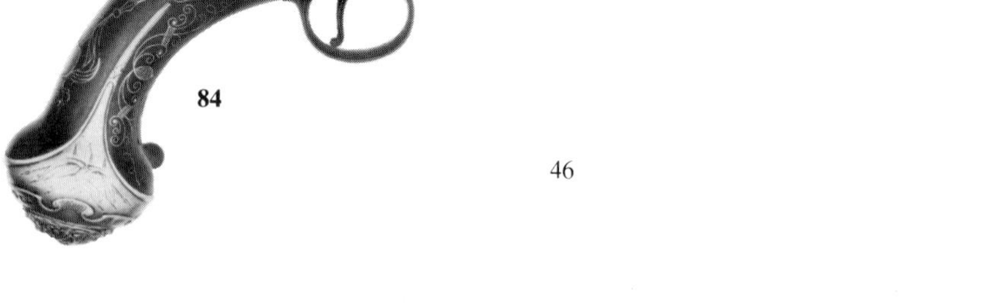

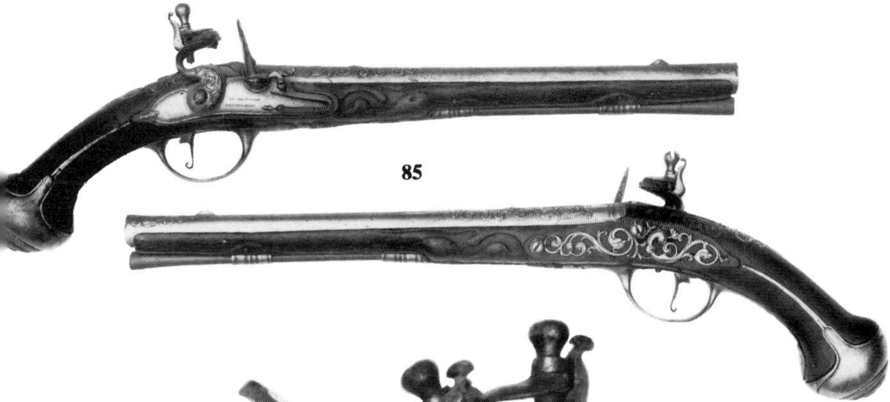

85

86

80 to 82. Made in about 1700, this pair of French flintlock pistols have rifled barrels which screw off. To prevent their loss the barrel is secured to the stock by an ingenious pivoted link. The locks are signed LANGUEDOC PARIS – a well known maker of quality as evidenced by the finely chiselled steel butt masks.

83 and 84. A fine example of a repeating flintlock pistol of the late eighteenth century by Wilson of London. The mechanism is of the pattern invented by Michele Lorenzoni of Florence in the seventeenth century. Magazines in the butt housed powder and balls. The lever at the side was connected to a circular breechblock. The pistol was held with the muzzle upright, the lever was rotated and this aligned two cavities with the magazines. The gun was tipped to deposit powder and ball into the cavities. The lever was rotated to deposit ball and powder into the breech. The same movement automatically primed and cocked the action. In good condition such rare pieces realize high prices.

85. Pair of Dutch holster pistols, late seventeenth century. The barrels are chiselled with scrolling foliage and masks as well as being struck with the Amsterdam town mark. The chiselled locks are signed JAN VAN SUILEN AMSTERDAM. The root walnut stocks are carved with scrolls and are fitted with steel furniture.

86. A mid eighteenth-century, all-steel flintlock boxlock pocket pistol signed L. MERCIER. The majority of these all-metal pistols are of Belgian origin including a number which carry spurious London marks. Many are single barrel whereas this example has two side-by-side barrels.

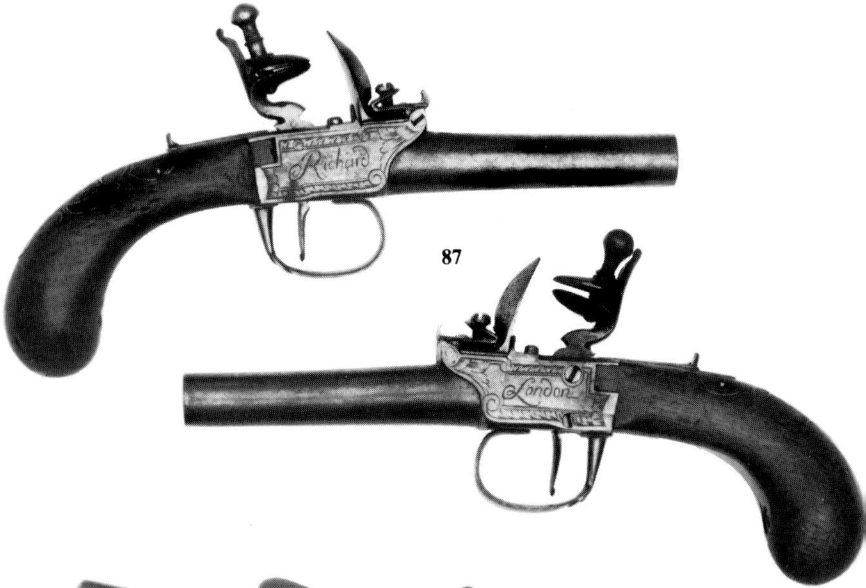

87

88

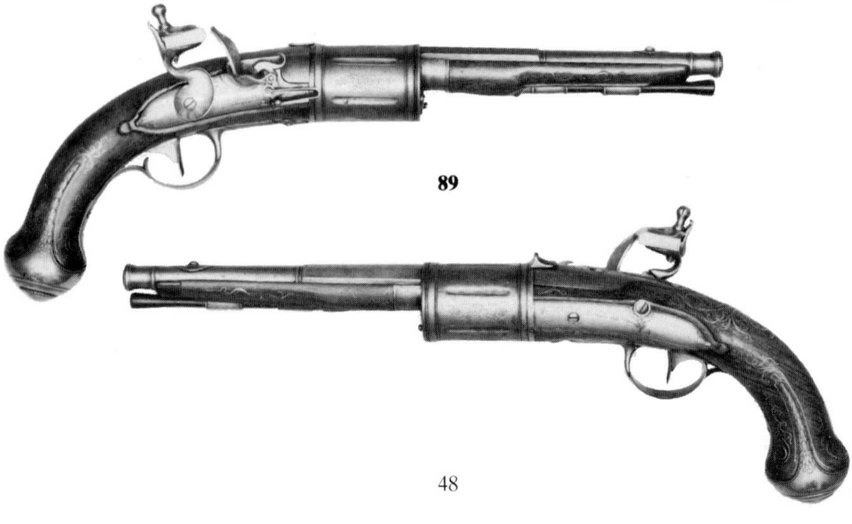

89

87. Although this pair of flintlock boxlock pocket pistols are signed RICHARD LONDON, they were made in Belgium in the late eighteenth century. Both have suffered some damage which would be reflected in their price.

88. Known as a ducksfoot pistol, these four-barrel weapons were offered as being very effective against attacking mobs. This one is signed H. NOCK and has a top sliding safety catch which locks the frizzen shut as well as locking the cock. Genuine ducksfoot pistols are rare and numerous copies are known.

89. A very rare pair of Russian flintlock revolvers, circa 1790. They are signed POLINSON LONDON although they were made by Ivan Polin who worked in the armoury at Tula from 1780 to 1810. The cylinders house chambers numbered 1–6.

90. An extremely rare and unusual breech-loading flintlock pistol. It was made and signed by JOSE DE ARMENTA who is recorded as working in Los Angeles early in the eighteenth century and he has adapted the Lorenzoni loading system (see Plates **83** and **84**) by using magazines for powder and ball placed along the barrel rather than in the butt. To load, the barrel assembly is turned to the right. Although the cock and butt have been restored, this is still a very rare and collectable item.

91. A pair of flintlock boxlock pocket pistols, circa 1820. The octagonal barrels are fitted with spring-operated bayonets and are struck at the breech with Liège proof marks. The trigger guards also serve as locking catches for the bayonets. The butts are chequered and have inlaid silver wire patterns.

90

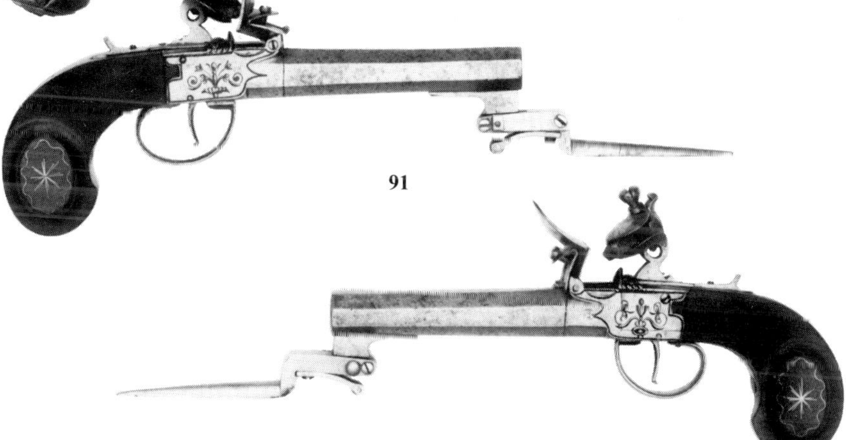

91

92

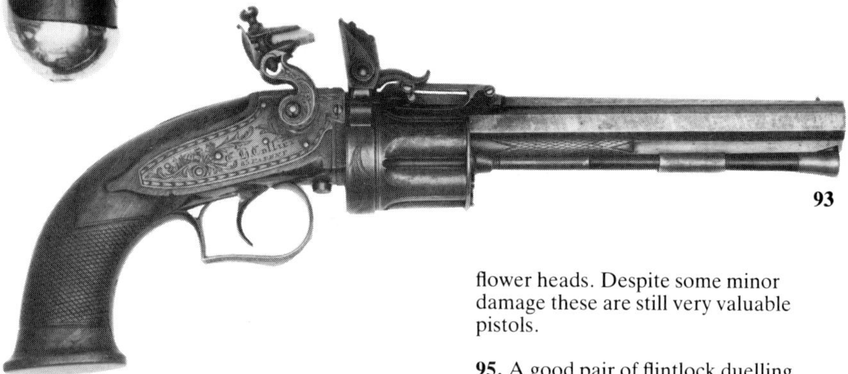

93

92. This French Cavalry pistol is known as the Model 1777 after the year in which it was officially adopted. The brass frame is inscribed ST. ETIENNE – the arsenal where it was made – and the butt is dated 1781. There is a belt hook because the pistol was intended primarily for use by the cavalry.

93. This is a good example of the rare Collier flintlock revolver, circa 1824. In 1818 Elisha Collier patented the revolver which originally had a hand-rotated cylinder. A spring was incorporated to rotate the cylinder, but it was apparently discarded and a self-priming frizzen was also adopted. Another novel feature was the forward movement of the cylinder to ensure a good tight fit against the breech end of the barrel.

94. A finely decorated pair of flintlock holster pistols, probably made in Silesia late in the seventeenth century. The barrels are blued and decorated overall with scrolls and leaves which were originally gilded. The locks and cocks have incised decoration and the stocks are inlaid with horn and mother-of-pearl engraved with monsters and flower heads. Despite some minor damage these are still very valuable pistols.

95. A good pair of flintlock duelling pistols, circa 1775, by Wogdon, the London maker who was renowned for this type of pistol. The flat-sided, rather hooked butts are typical of this maker's duelling pistols. This pair have had the barrels re-browned and some 'refreshing' has been carried out. The effect is to reduce the value to collectors but they would still be quite expensive.

96. An officer's pair of flintlock pistols, circa 1770, the barrels bearing London proof marks and the maker's mark RW. The locks are signed WILSON and the iron furniture has some simple incised decoration.

97. A good pair of flintlock duelling pistols, circa 1800, by H. W. Mortimer. They were at some time in Ireland for the barrels are stamped with Irish census marks for Dublin. In 1843 an Act of Parliament decreed that weapons in Ireland should be registered with the police and they were then stamped with a number and letters identifying the place of registration. The pistols, which are cased, have accessories in good condition and retain some original colouring, making them attractive to collectors.

94

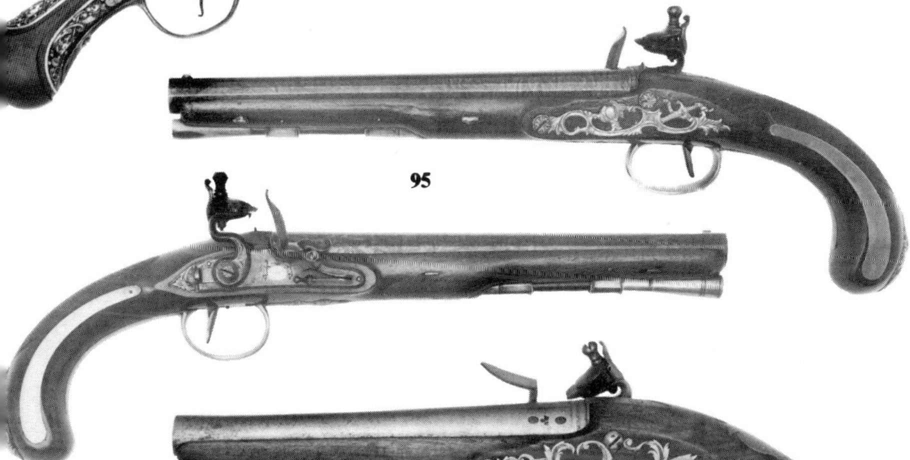

95

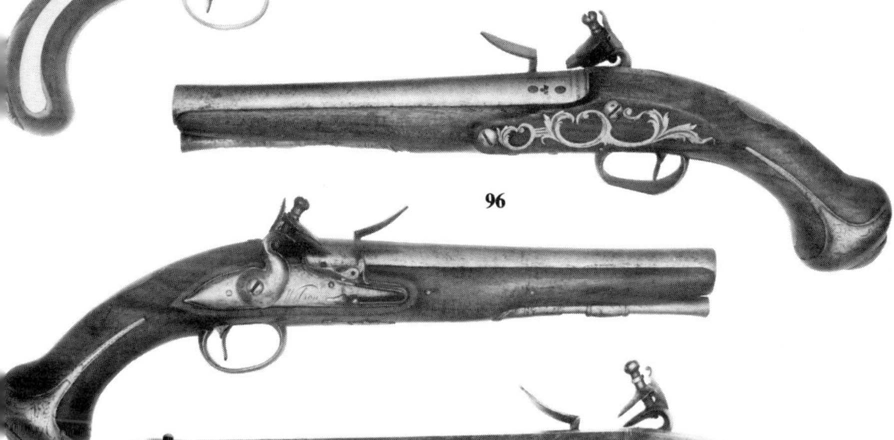

96

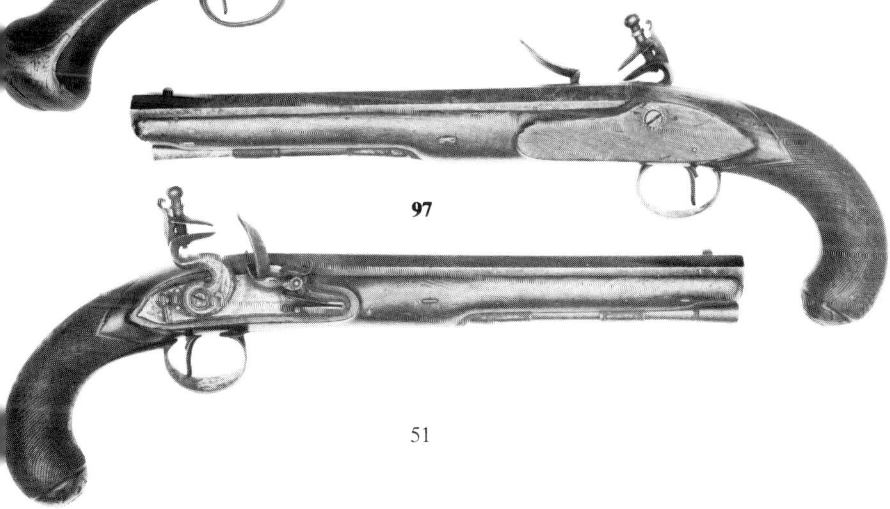

97

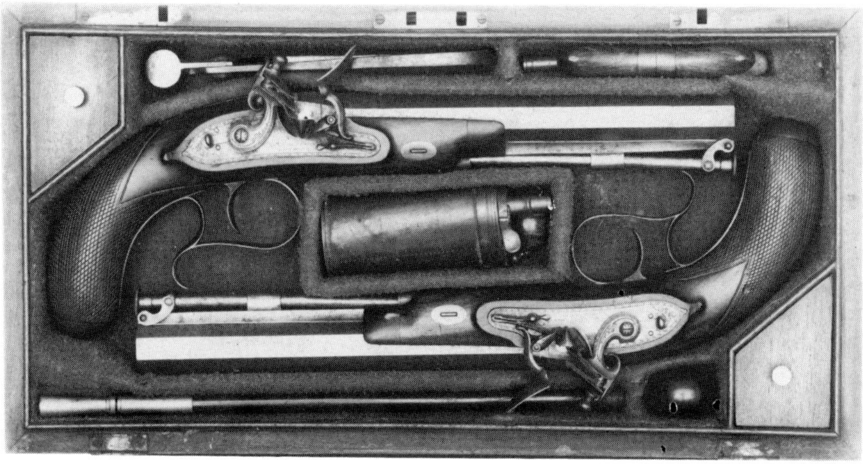

98

99

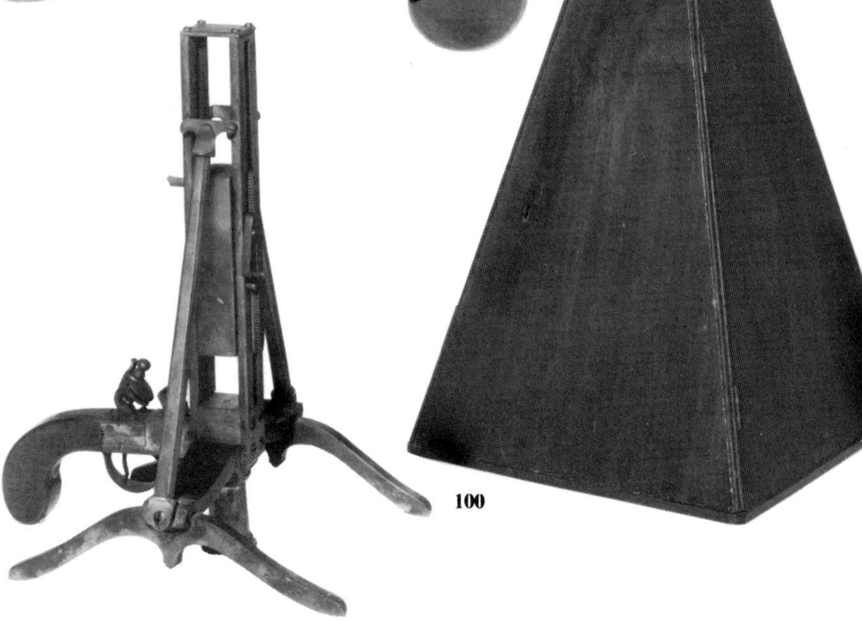

100

101

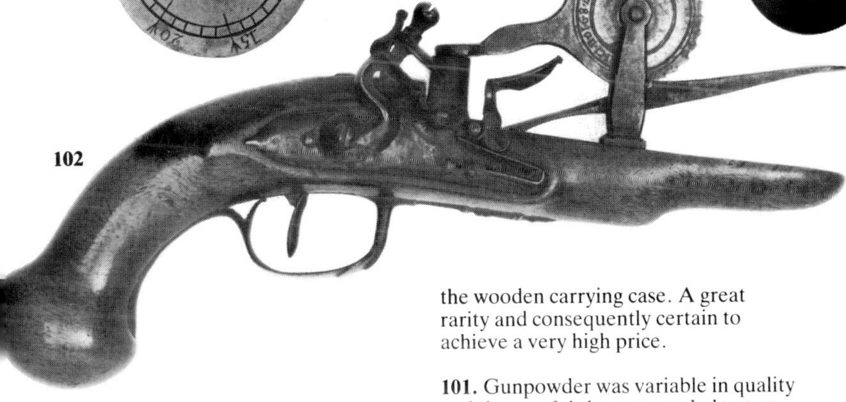

102

98. Pair of officer's or duelling pistols, circa 1815, by Alexander Wilson of London. They incorporate all the features of late, good-quality locks, with platinum vents, rain-proof pans, and roller bearing on the toe of the frizzen. The case is not the original and has the trade label of another London maker, William Bond, and this would reduce the value of the set.

99. Tinder-lighter, the brass frame signed E. BOND, LONDON, the butt with some chequering and silver escutcheon.

100. This elaborate *éprouvette* by Mortimer of St. James's Street, London, dates from the early nineteenth century and is possibly unique. The flintlock pistol section is conventional, but the rest is far more elaborate with a complex brass measure. Another unusual feature is the wooden carrying case. A great rarity and consequently certain to achieve a very high price.

101. Gunpowder was variable in quality and the careful shooter needed to test each batch to check its power. *Eprouvettes* or powder testers were designed to measure the thrust of a measured charge and they will be found fitted with matchlock, flintlock and percussion-cap ignition systems. This flintlock *éprouvette* by Simmons has a measuring wheel marked off with 25 divisions. A charge of powder was placed in the pan and fired in the normal fashion. The expanding gas pushed against the projecting arm which covered the muzzle of the 'barrel', causing the 'wheel' to rotate. Obviously the degree of rotation measured on the scale on the 'wheel' gave a good indication of the powder's relative power.

102. French *éprouvette*, eighteenth century. The powder was contained in the tubular compartment above the lock, the top covered by the tip of the arm of the wheel.

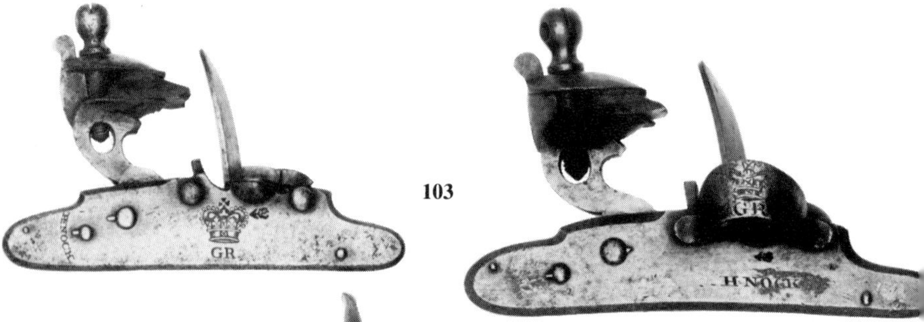

103

104

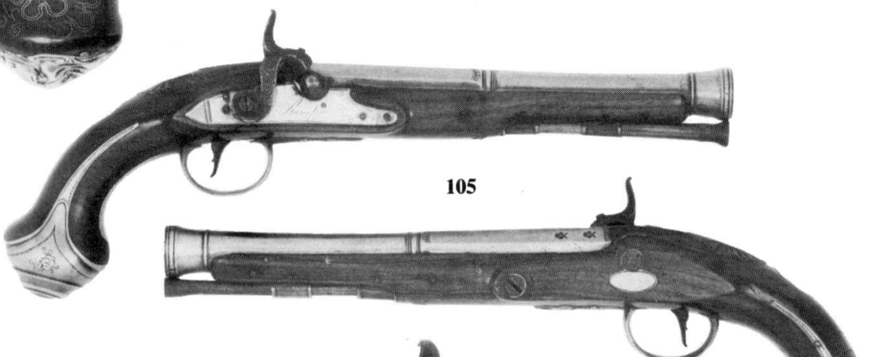

105

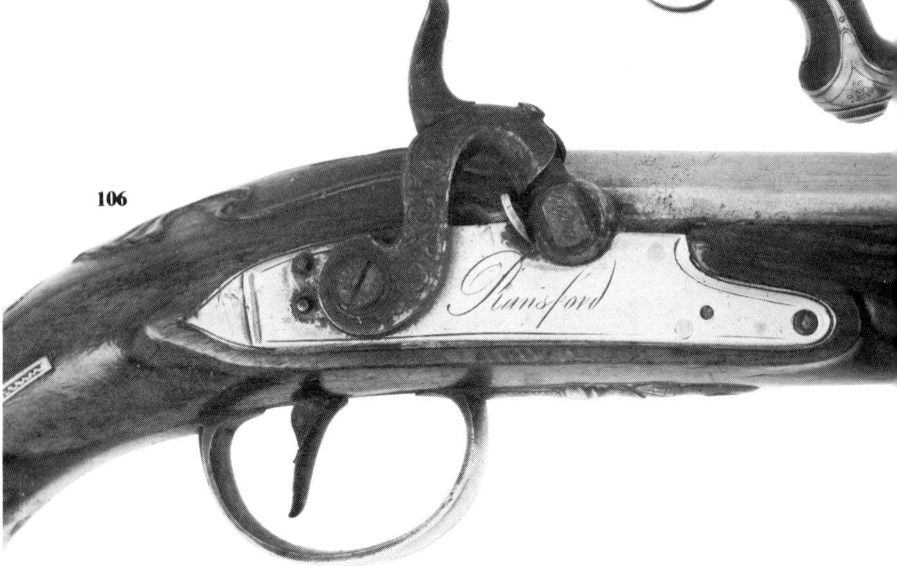

106

107

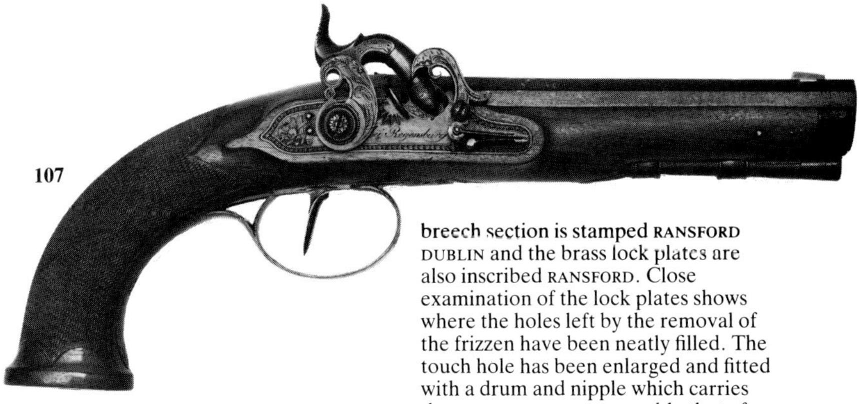

103. Henry Nock, a versatile and prolific London gunmaker, designed a lock which used no screws to hold it together. It was produced in a number of slightly variant designs – some with covers around the pan – others without. Such locks will be found fitted on both pistols and longarms.

104. A double-barrel flintlock boxlock pocket pistol, circa 1775, has been converted to the new percussion-cap system, circa 1820. The frizzen has been removed and nipples inserted in the touch holes, while the cock has been replaced by a hammer with a disc which was turned to strike one nipple or the other. The silver decorated pistol was originally made by Bunney of London.

105 and 106. A pair of Irish percussion-cap pistols converted from flintlock, with brass barrels belling slightly at the muzzles. The top flat of the octagonal breech section is stamped RANSFORD DUBLIN and the brass lock plates are also inscribed RANSFORD. Close examination of the lock plates shows where the holes left by the removal of the frizzen have been neatly filled. The touch hole has been enlarged and fitted with a drum and nipple which carries the name BAILEY, presumably that of the converter. The pistols date from about 1750, but the conversion would most likely have been carried out in about 1820–30.

107. One of a pair of rifled travelling pistols converted to the percussion system from flintlock. It was made early in the nineteenth century by a member of a very famous gunmaking family from Regensburg, Johann Christoph Kuchenreuter (1755–1818). Long-nosed hammers have been substituted for the cock and the frizzen has been replaced. This is one of a pair contained in their original

108. A simple percussion-cap overcoat pistol of about 1840, reduced to its basic components. Note the method of securing the barrel to the stock using a rectangular lug below the barrel which is engaged by the rectangular wedge passing through the stock.

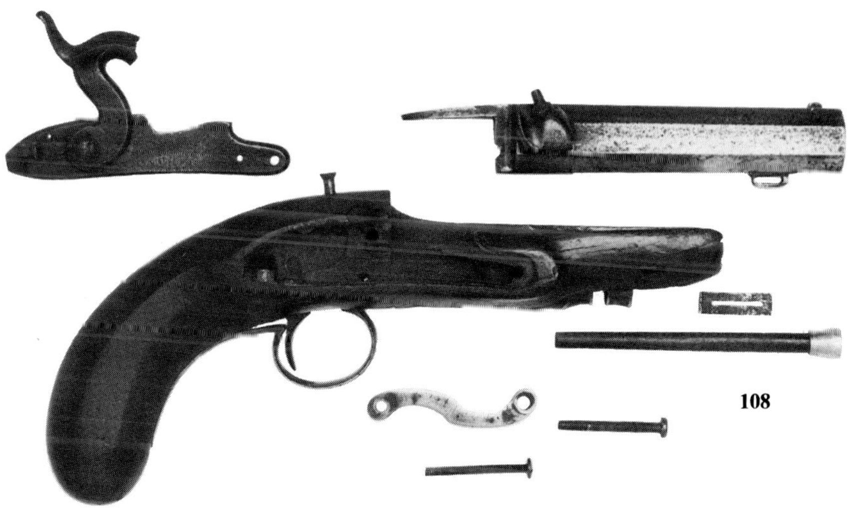

108

109

110

111

112

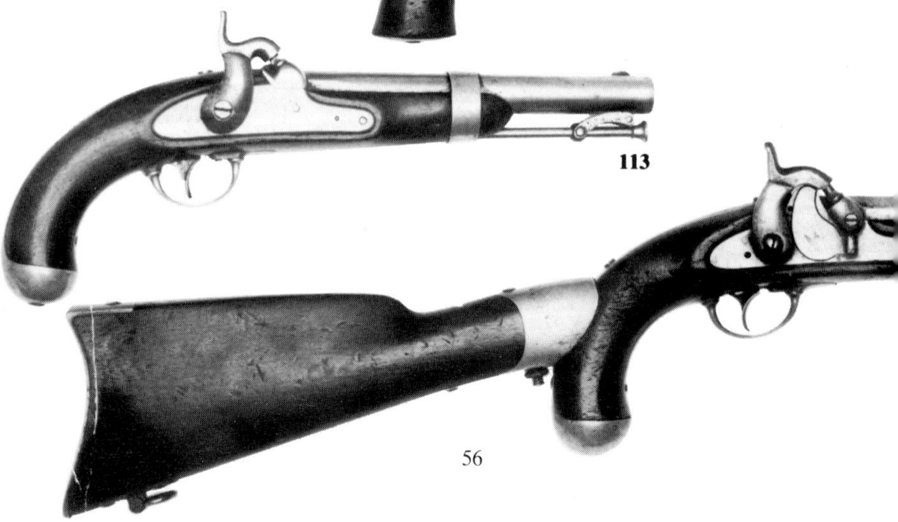

113

115

109. A coastguard percussion-cap pistol of about 1850. This is an example of the lower end of the antique pistol market; the metal work is pitted and the ramrod is missing. In this condition it would sell cheaply, but before such pieces are purchased it is worth considering what the prospects are. It is now possible to replace missing parts fairly easily and no doubt the metal work can be improved, but when finished this pistol will be fairly heavily restored and as such the value will not be greatly increased.

110. A US Model 1836 flintlock pistol, the barrel stamped U.S. J.H.P. and the lock U.S. R. JOHNSON MIDDN CONN. 1842. This model pistol was made from 1836–1844 and saw service in the Mexican War.

111. A US Model 1842 percussion-cap pistol. The barrel tang is stamped with the date of manufacture. The lock is stamped U.S. H. ASTON MIDDTN. CONN. 1849. Aston was an Englishman who went to work for Simeon North, a famous American maker.

111

112. A US Navy Model 1842 percussion-cap pistol, the barrel is stamped U.S.N. 1844 R.P.P. and the lock is signed N. P. AMES SPRINGFIELD MASS. The hammer is mounted so that part is covered by the lock plate.

113. A US Model 1842 percussion-cap pistol made by William Glaze & Co. of Columbia, South Carolina. The lock is stamped with a palm tree and PALMETTO ARMORY S.C. and S. COLUMBIA SC 1852. These pistols were originally made under contract for South Carolina.

114. A US Pistol Carbine, Model 1855. The 12-inch barrel is rifled with three grooves and the lock is fitted with a Maynard cap primer. The fulminate compound was mounted as small priming caps on a narrow strip of paper which was moved on as the hammer was cocked and was then positioned above the nipple. The shoulder stock was detachable.

115. One of a pair of percussion-cap travelling pistols, circa 1840. They retain much original colour and are slightly unusual in having the top-mounted spring bayonet. The pistols were made by I. Blissett of Leadenhall Street, London.

116

116. Percussion-cap Scottish dress pistols, circa 1830, with blued, engraved barrels signed PATTON & WALSH PERTH. The silver stocks are also engraved with scrolls and leaves and the butts are set with cairngorms. A very decorative if somewhat damaged pair.

117. A cased pair of double-barrel percussion pistols by C. Lancaster of New Bond Street, London, circa 1840. The engraved frames are fitted with sliding safety catches which lock the hammers in the half-cock position. The oak case has most of the accessories, but the powder flask is probably associated.

118. A pair of side-by-side, double-barrel percussion travelling pistols, circa 1840. The browned twist barrels are signed WITTON, DAW & CO. 57, THREADNEEDLE STREET and the chequered butts are fitted with traps with hinged lids.

119. Pair of Scottish percussion-cap pistols, circa 1830. Made by the famous London maker, Mortimer, they were intended as costume pieces rather than serious weapons. They are in very good condition and retain much of their original colouring.

120. Pair of boxlock percussion-cap pistols, circa 1840, by Adkin of Bedford – as a pair they are likely to realize more than twice the cost of a single pistol.

121. This mid nineteenth-century percussion-cap pistol has an internal hammer which strikes the nipple fitted at the breech end of a pivoted barrel. It is probably French although there are no names or marks to identify its country of origin.

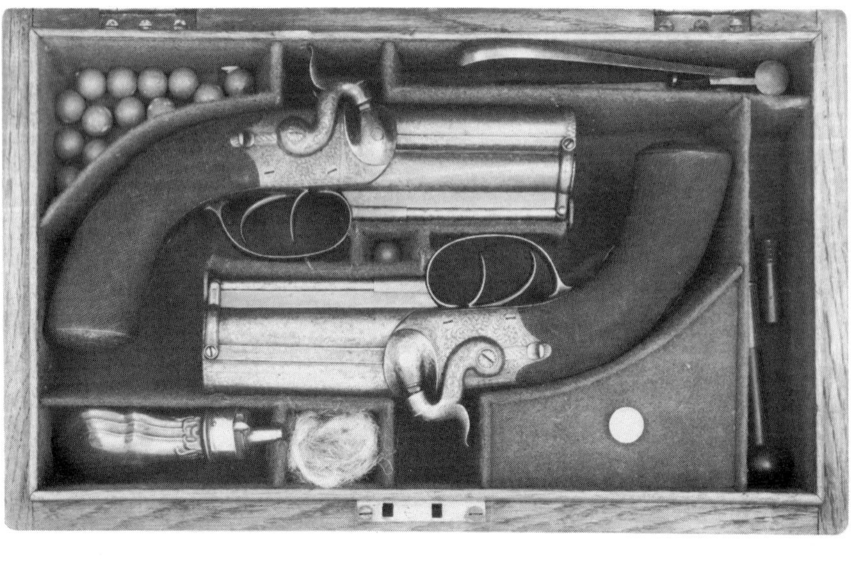

1

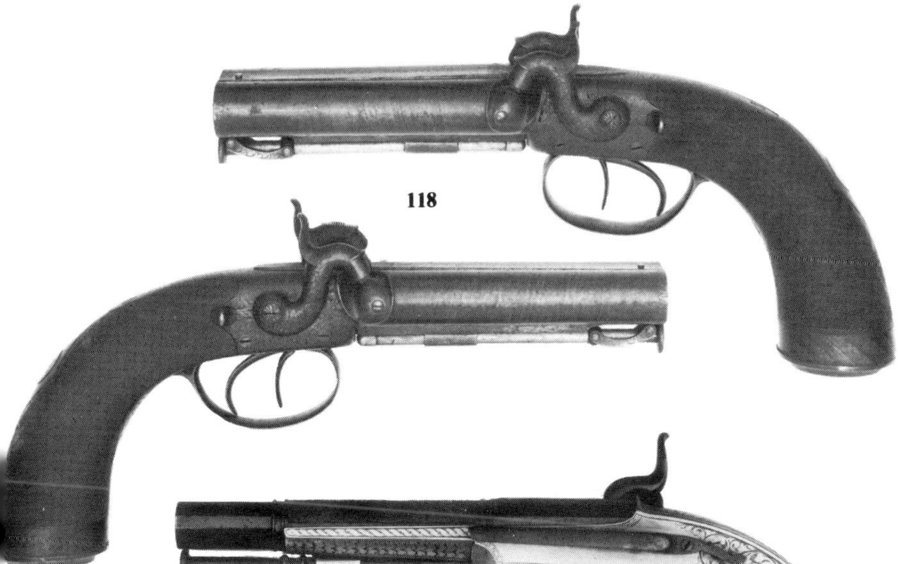

118

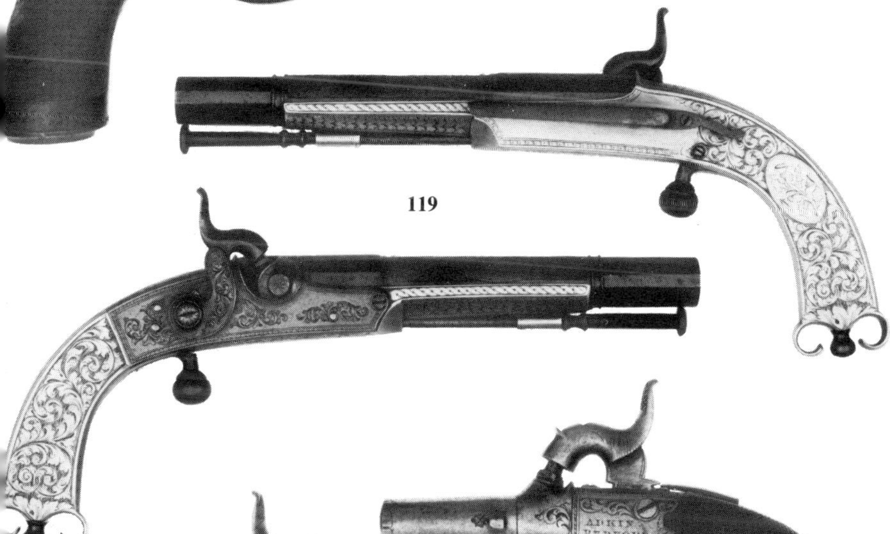

119

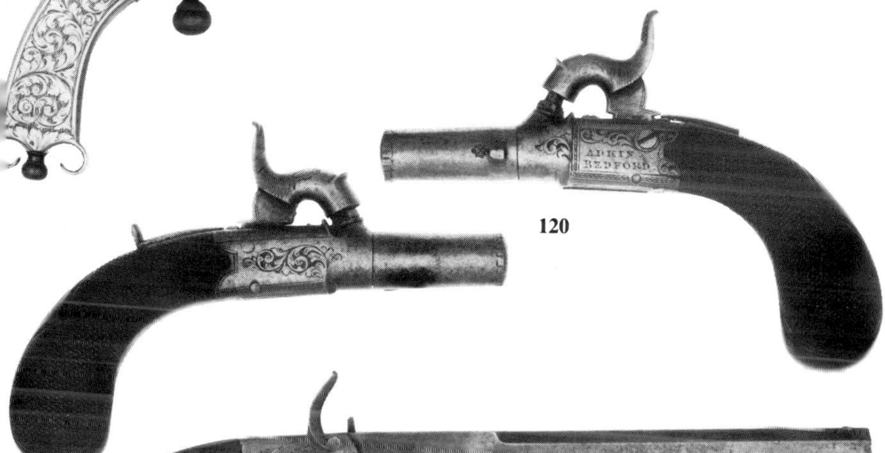

120

121

122

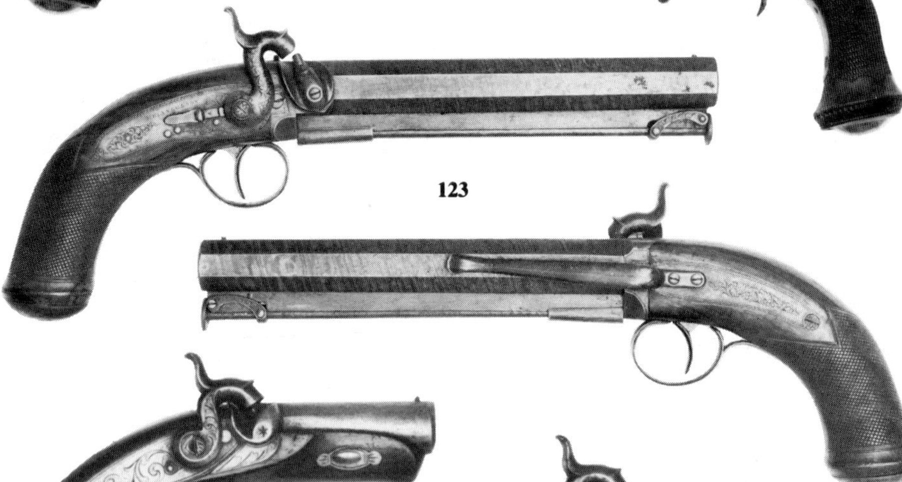

123

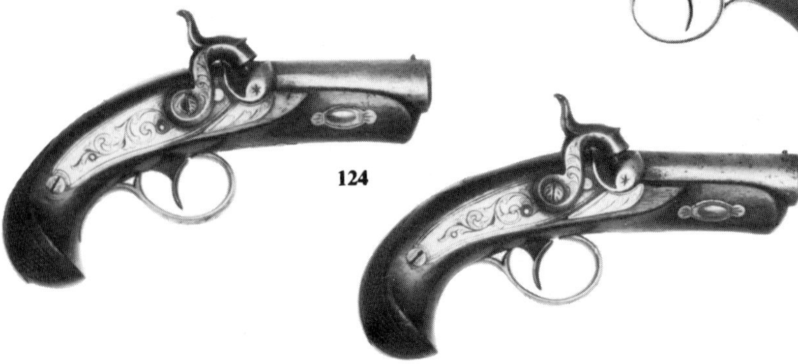

124

125

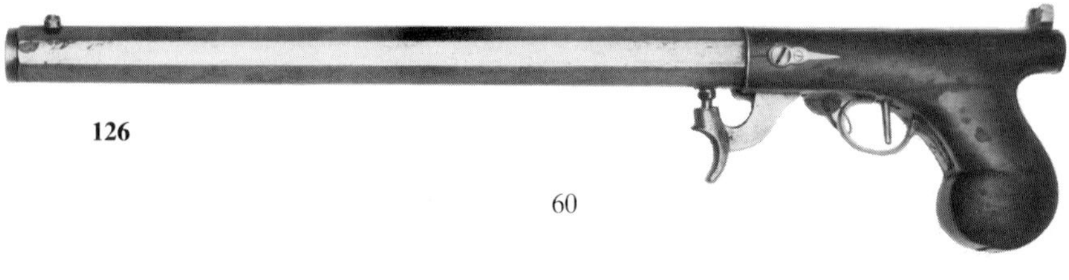

126

127

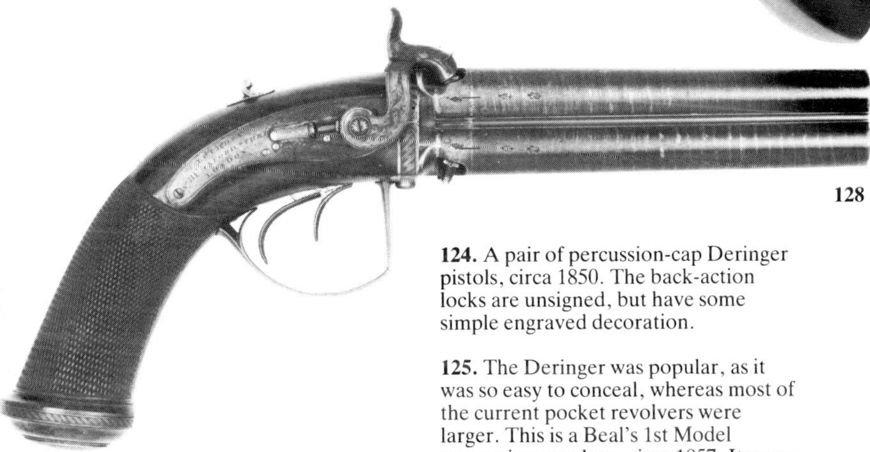

128

122. A pair of underhammer percussion-cap pistols, circa 1840, and of French manufacture. The long octagonal Damascus barrels are stamped PAR BREVET JBC and carry St. Etienne proof marks. Advantages of this style of fitting are mechanical simplicity and an uncluttered sight line along the barrel.

123. A pair of percussion-cap travelling pistols by J. Blanch & Son, London, circa 1830–50. The long octagonal barrels retain some original colour and are signed by the maker. The locks are back action which means that the spring is fitted behind the tumbler rather than in the more conventional position in front. Safety catches push forward to engage with the rear of the hammer. Running along the side of the barrels are the belt hooks.

124. A pair of percussion-cap Deringer pistols, circa 1850. The back-action locks are unsigned, but have some simple engraved decoration.

125. The Deringer was popular, as it was so easy to conceal, whereas most of the current pocket revolvers were larger. This is a Beal's 1st Model percussion revolver, circa 1857. It was a five-shot weapon of .31 calibre made by Remington.

126. A target pistol with an underhammer lock and an exceptionally long octagonal barrel stamped J. I. EASTMAN CONCORD N.H. 1866.

127. A Bootleg pistol, circa 1840, with an underhammer lock. It has a brass frame and an octagonal barrel stamped W. ASHTON.

128. Superb quality and condition make this four-barrelled percussion-cap pistol by L. Purdey of 314½ Oxford Street, circa 1840, very desirable. The two uppermost barrels were fired and the barrel assembly unlocked by a catch mounted on the tang and rotated to bring the lower barrels into the firing position.

129

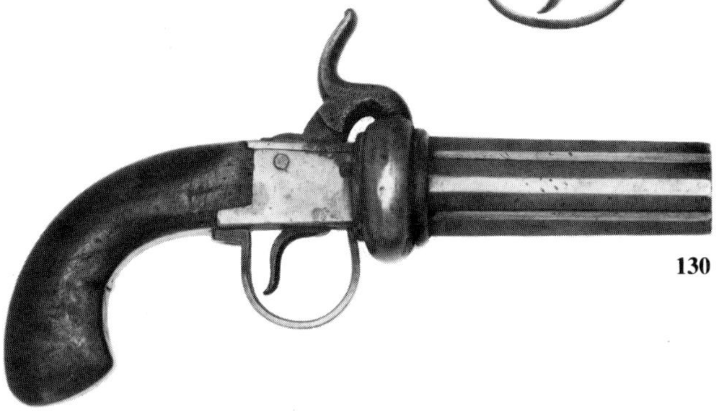

130

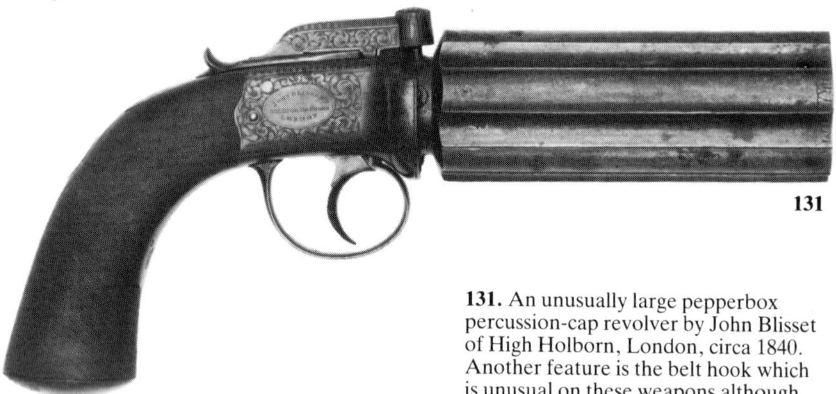

131

131. An unusually large pepperbox percussion-cap revolver by John Blisset of High Holborn, London, circa 1840. Another feature is the belt hook which is unusual on these weapons although they were sometimes carried in leather holsters.

129. A conventional but good quality percussion-cap pepperbox revolver, circa 1840–50, made by W. Tranter who was later to specialize in percussion revolvers.

130. An uncommon percussion-cap pepperbox with four octagonal barrels, probably Scandinavian in origin. The frame is of brass and the action is very simple since the barrel assembly is hand rotated – probably circa 1840.

132. A cased percussion-cap pepperbox revolver by W. Parker, circa 1840. The engraved nickel-silver frame is engraved IMPROVED REVOLVING PISTOL. The accessories include a small powder flask, ramrod and a key for unscrewing the nipples.

133. Cased percussion-cap pepperbox revolver, circa 1840 – the lid with trade label of Parker Field. In good general condition.

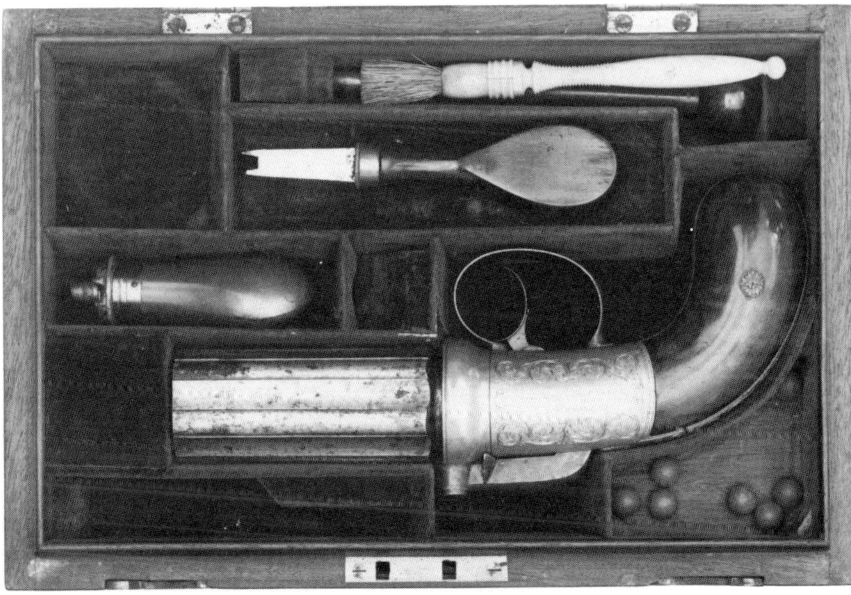

132

133

134

135

134. A transition percussion-cap revolver by the London gunmaker, T. K. Baker, numbered 1496, circa 1840. This model has an unusual hammer which allows it to be cocked manually.

135. A fairly typical Birmingham-made transition revolver of the mid nineteenth century. It is self-cocking, the hammer being cocked and released by pressure on the trigger alone. This specimen is a little unusual in having a lanyard ring fitted to the butt.

136. Transitional percussion-cap revolvers are usually fairly basic, but this example by T & F Roper of Halifax, circa 1850, is of superior design. The cylinder is fluted and there is a spring-loaded ramrod mounted beneath the barrel. It also has an automatic safety catch which engages when the trigger is first put under pressure. The case with its accessories naturally increases its value.

137. A transitional percussion-cap revolver, circa 1840. The cylinder bears London proof marks while the butt has a rather Continental style of decoration. The weapon is also unusual in having a large hammer spur; there is also a sliding safety catch at the top of the butt.

138. One of the rarest of all the Colt percussion-cap revolvers, a .44 Whitneyville Walker Dragoon. This was the type issued to the early Texas Rangers and its rarity ensures that any decent example will realize a very high price. However there are far more copies than originals!

139. A Third Model Colt Dragoon .44 percussion-cap revolver. This is of particular interest since the butt bears a small pewter heart. This would suggest that the revolver was used by the 24th Corps during the American Civil War; the heart was the Corps' badge. (Private Collection)

136

137

138

139

140

141

142

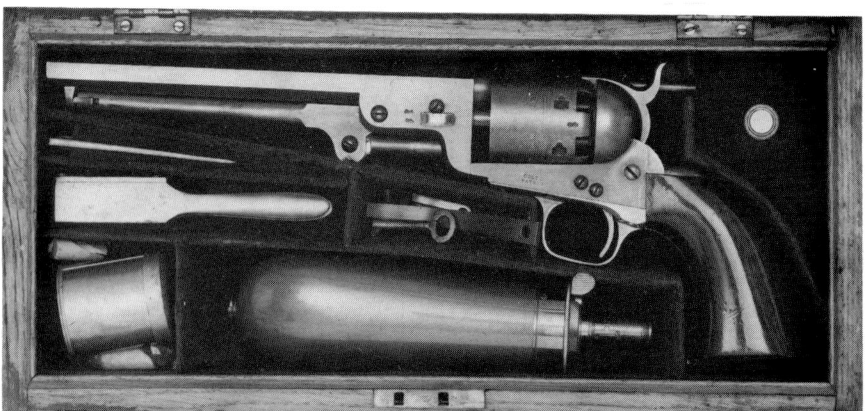

1

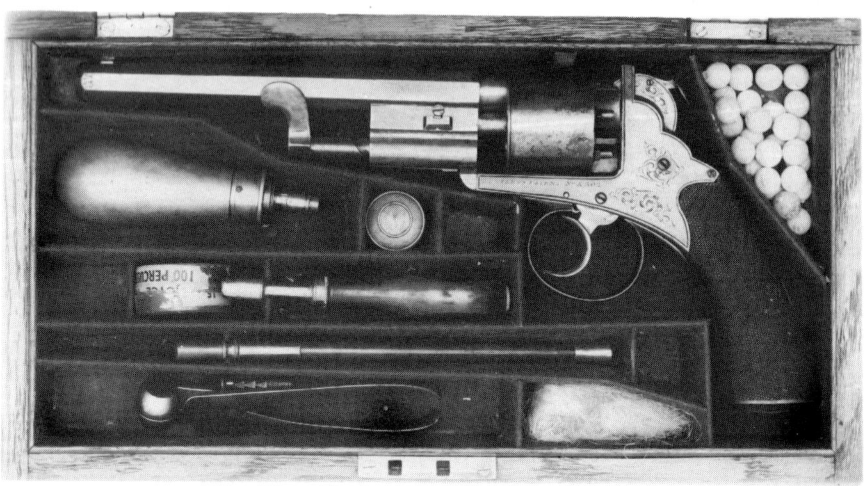

1

145

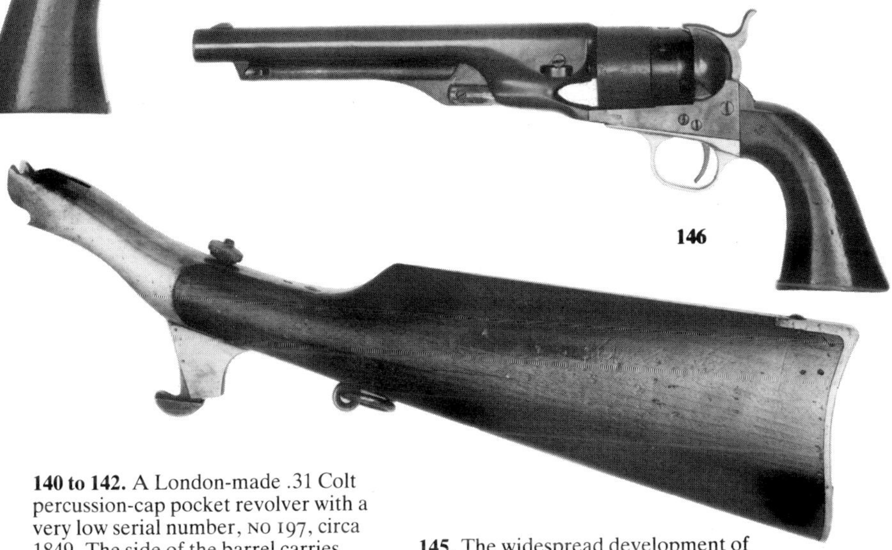

146

140 to 142. A London-made .31 Colt percussion-cap pocket revolver with a very low serial number, NO 197, circa 1849. The side of the barrel carries London proof marks and the top flat is stamped with the London address. Colt revolvers are normally numbered on the cylinder, trigger guard, frame and butt strap. Revolvers with all parts carrying the same number are more desirable than those with mixed numbers. The low serial number on this example would increase its value.

143. An unusually attractive cased London .36 Colt Navy percussion-cap revolver. The weapon retains some of the original colouring – always a desirable feature – and is in its original case with most of the accessories.

144. Another English percussion-cap revolver, circa 1858. This cased example is inscribed JOHN CALVERT LEEDS on the octagonal barrel and BENTLEY'S PATENT NO. A 502 on the frame. One distinctive feature is the spring-loaded ramrod which operates on a 'screw' principle, having a deep cut spiral groove.

145. The widespread development of cartridges led to the introduction of many designs for converting percussion-cap revolvers to their use. This Colt .44 1860 Army percussion-cap revolver has been converted, circa 1871–72, to take a centrefire cartridge by adapting the cylinder and frame to take a loading gate and lengthening the nose of the hammer to serve as a firing pin. The loading lever has been replaced by an ejector rod to force out the empty cases. The value in Britain is restricted because it is a weapon which can only be possessed by the holder of an appropriate Firearm Certificate.

146. In 1861 Samuel Colt produced the .44 Colt Army revolver with its toothed 'creeping' ramrod below the barrel. Many had features which enabled them to be fitted with a detachable stock which converted the revolver to a carbine. A genuine stock enhances the value of the revolver many times, but there are numerous modern copies on the market.

147

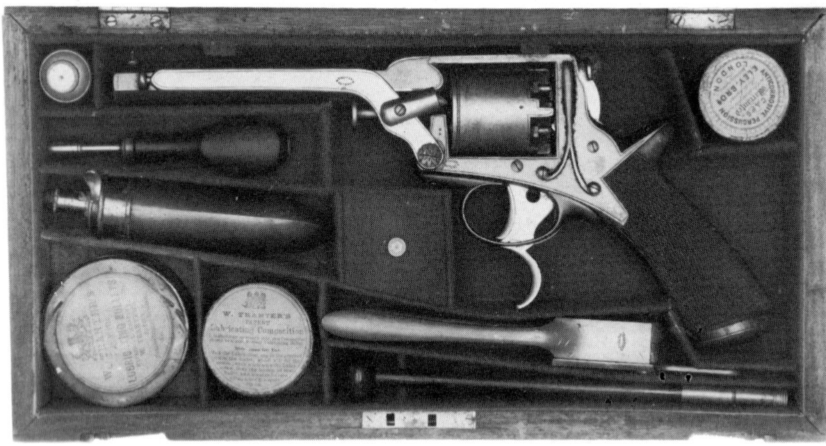

148

147. Cased Tranter percussion-cap revolver, No. 21286 T, by Jno Rigby of London. In very good condition with much original colour and many accessories.

148. A cased William Tranter double trigger percussion-cap revolver, circa 1860. Tranter sought to combine the accuracy of single-action fire with the speed of double action.

149. Tranter's double trigger, percussion-cap revolvers were designed so that pressure on the lower trigger rotated the cylinder and cocked the hammer. The revolver could then be held in this condition until the second trigger, housed within the guard, was

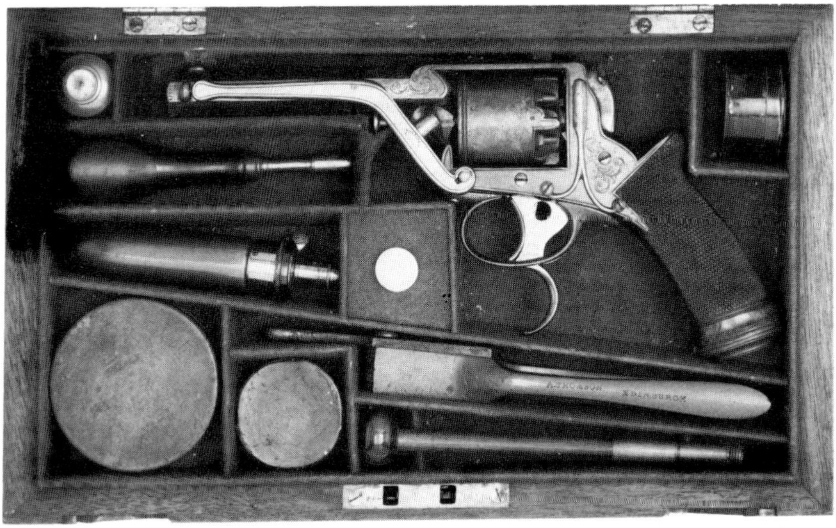

149

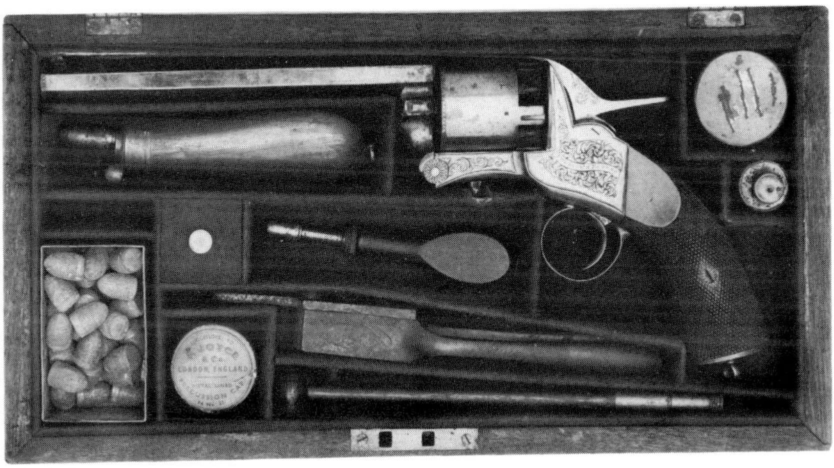

150

given only a touch to fire the shot. This system overcame the heavy pull normally required to cock and fire a revolver in one movement which had made it difficult to fire rapid shots. This cased example, retailed by Alexander Thomson, 16, Union Place, Edinburgh, is numbered 1564T and is unusual in having a mould stamped with the supplier's name.

150. A cased Webley percussion-cap revolver, circa 1855. The characteristic shape to the hammer has given this model the name 'Long spur Webley'. The case holds the correct accessories including some spare nipples. The revolver is five shot and .45 calibre; the hammer has a notch cut in its nose to serve as a rear sight in the same way as on Colt revolvers.

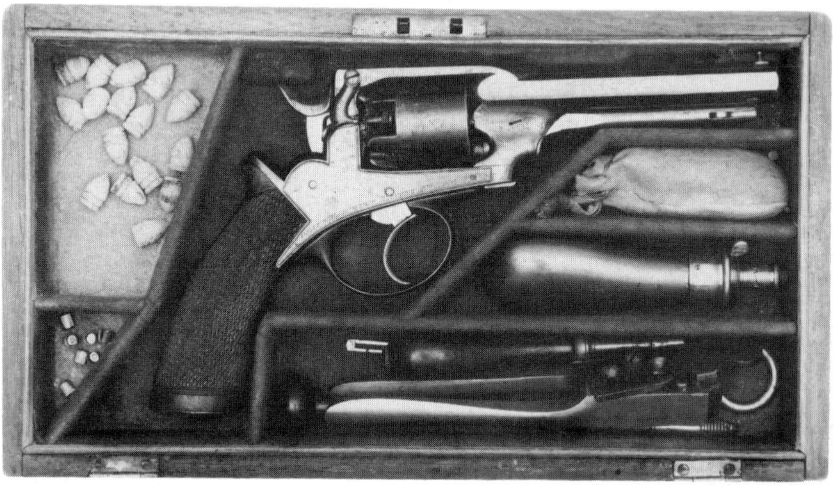

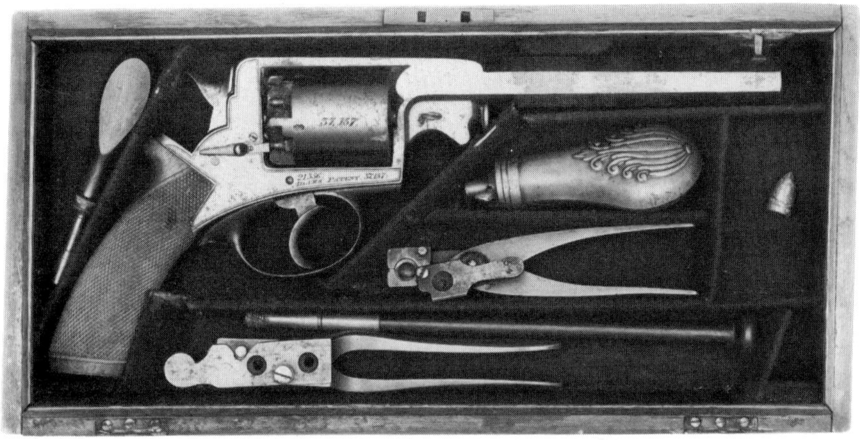

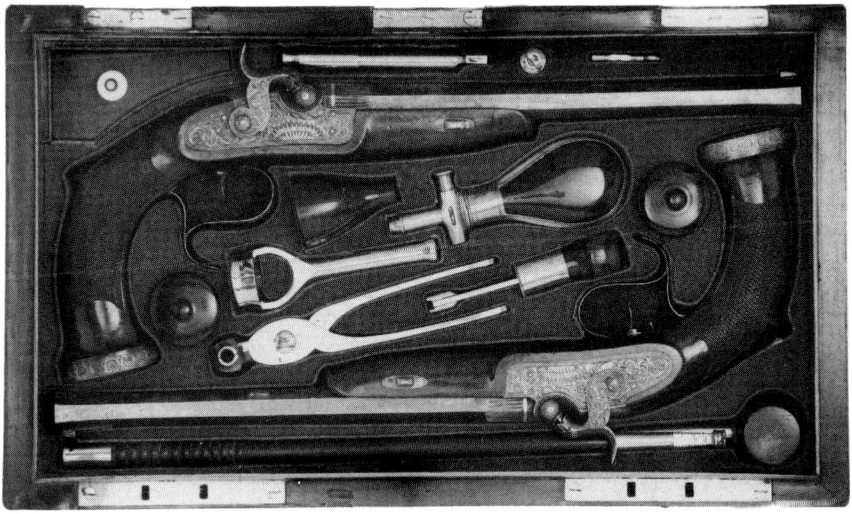

154

151. Another English percussion-cap revolver by Deane Harding, circa 1860. It has an under-barrel rammer like Colt revolvers. An unusual hook-shaped safety catch is mounted at the top of the frame, but its main feature was its two-part frame in which the barrel could be pivoted forward allowing the cylinder to be removed for cleaning.

155

152. A cased Beaumont Adams percussion-cap revolver of the mid nineteenth century. The feature of this weapon was its ability to be operated as a self-cocker, i.e., operated solely by the action of the trigger or by first cocking the hammer manually. The accessories are mixed, some being associated.

153. Another example of the many English percussion-cap revolvers which flourished during the mid nineteenth century. This one is of a design patented by John Kerr in 1858 and intended to be of the simplest construction so that any gunsmith could repair and maintain it. Its most noticeable feature is the externally-mounted side hammer. The revolver is cased with most of its accessories.

154 and 155. A fine cased set of rifled, percussion-cap target pistols by Contriner of Ingollersdorf. The pistols have the maker's name inlaid in gold as well as some decorative inlay. The set of the butt is unusual and designed for a firm, comfortable grip, and the back sight is adjustable. The style of rifling is unusual, consisting of sets of three grooves spaced equi-distant around the barrel. The red-and-green lined case is in the Continental style with contoured compartments for the accessories.

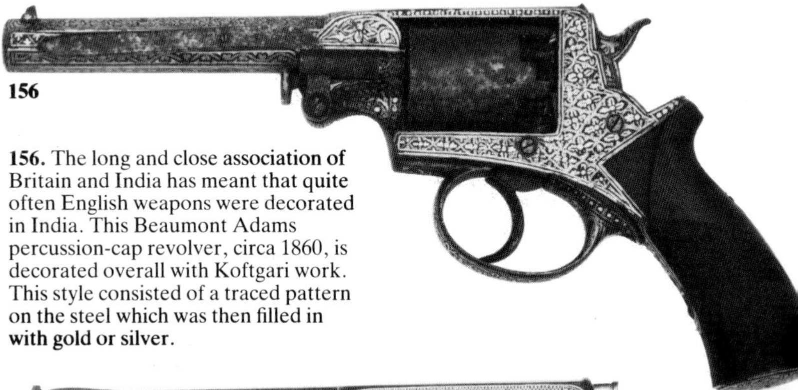

156

156. The long and close association of Britain and India has meant that quite often English weapons were decorated in India. This Beaumont Adams percussion-cap revolver, circa 1860, is decorated overall with Koftgari work. This style consisted of a traced pattern on the steel which was then filled in with gold or silver.

157

157. A similar piece, of better quality and condition. In this revolver the entire hammer has been gilded.

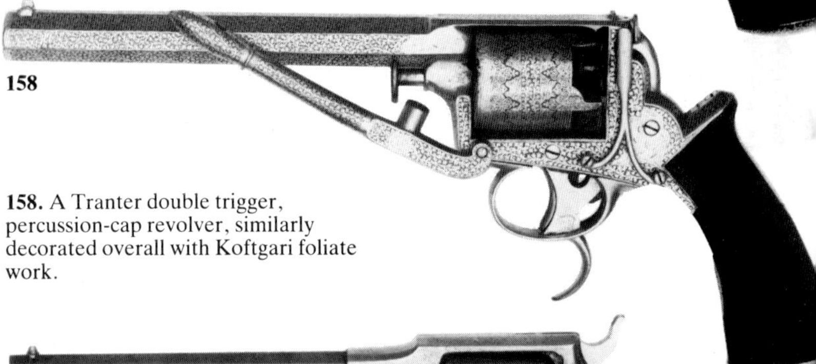

158

158. A Tranter double trigger, percussion-cap revolver, similarly decorated overall with Koftgari foliate work.

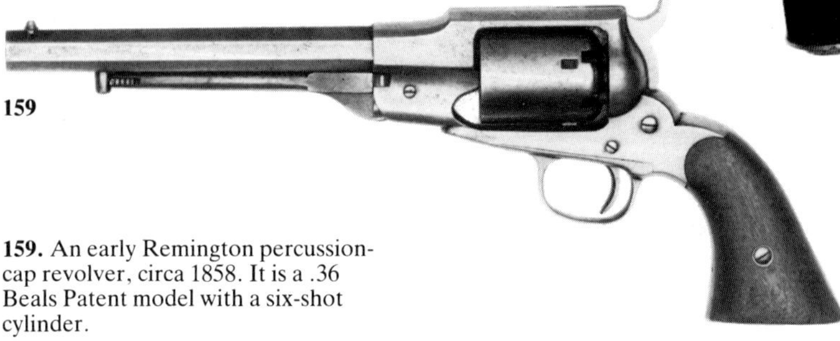

159

159. An early Remington percussion-cap revolver, circa 1858. It is a .36 Beals Patent model with a six-shot cylinder.

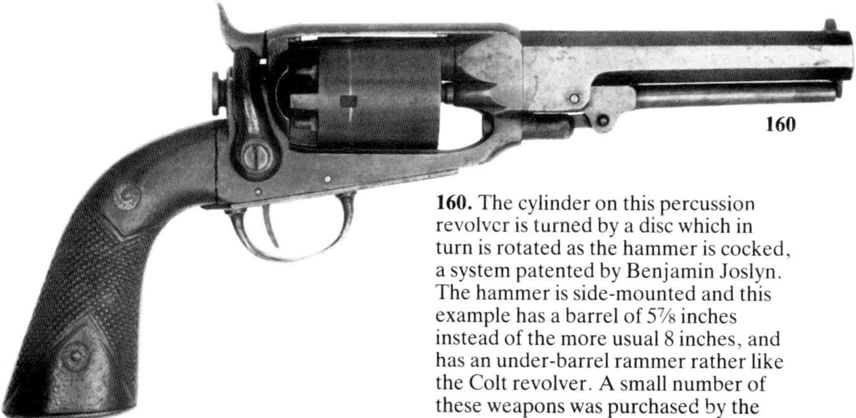

160

160. The cylinder on this percussion revolver is turned by a disc which in turn is rotated as the hammer is cocked, a system patented by Benjamin Joslyn. The hammer is side-mounted and this example has a barrel of 5⅞ inches instead of the more usual 8 inches, and has an under-barrel rammer rather like the Colt revolver. A small number of these weapons was purchased by the US Government in the 1860s.

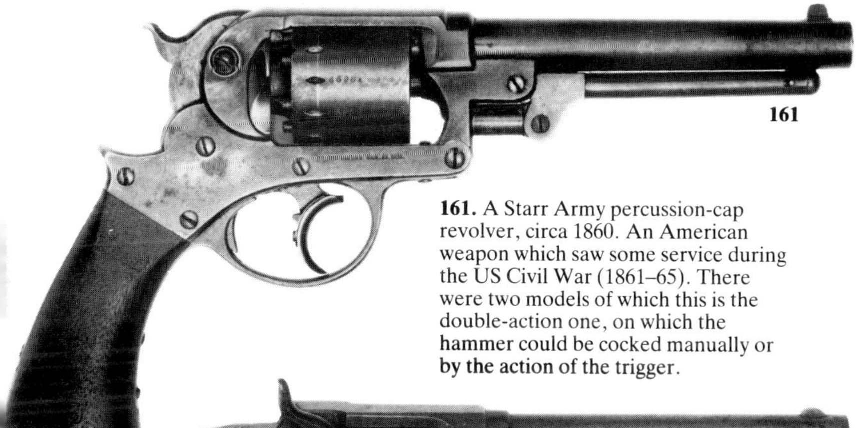

161

161. A Starr Army percussion-cap revolver, circa 1860. An American weapon which saw some service during the US Civil War (1861–65). There were two models of which this is the double-action one, on which the hammer could be cocked manually or by the action of the trigger.

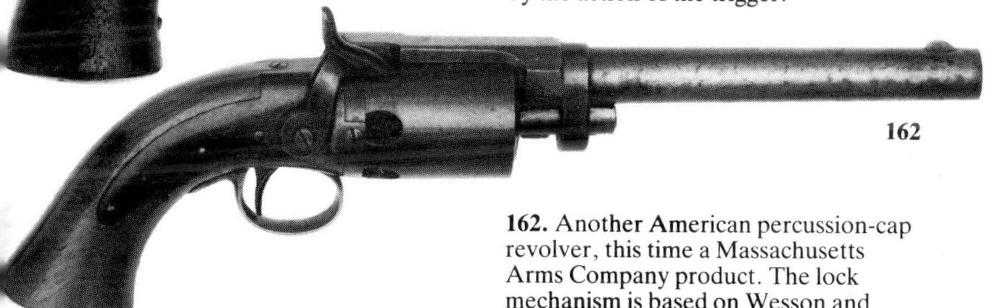

162

162. Another American percussion-cap revolver, this time a Massachusetts Arms Company product. The lock mechanism is based on Wesson and Levett's patent and uses a back-action lock.

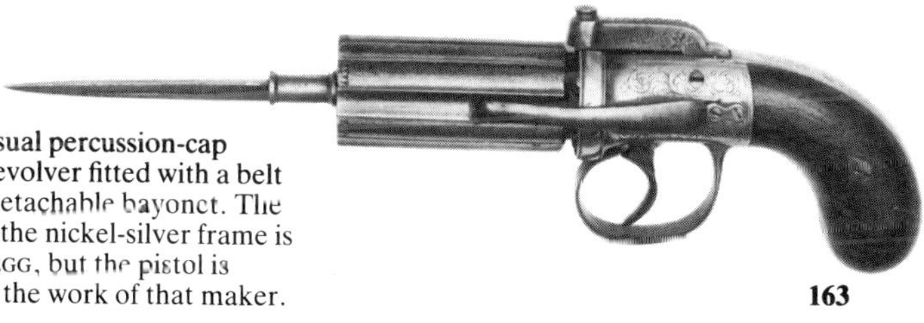

163

163. An unusual percussion-cap pepperbox revolver fitted with a belt hook and a detachable bayonet. The backstrap of the nickel-silver frame is inscribed D.EGG, but the pistol is certainly not the work of that maker.

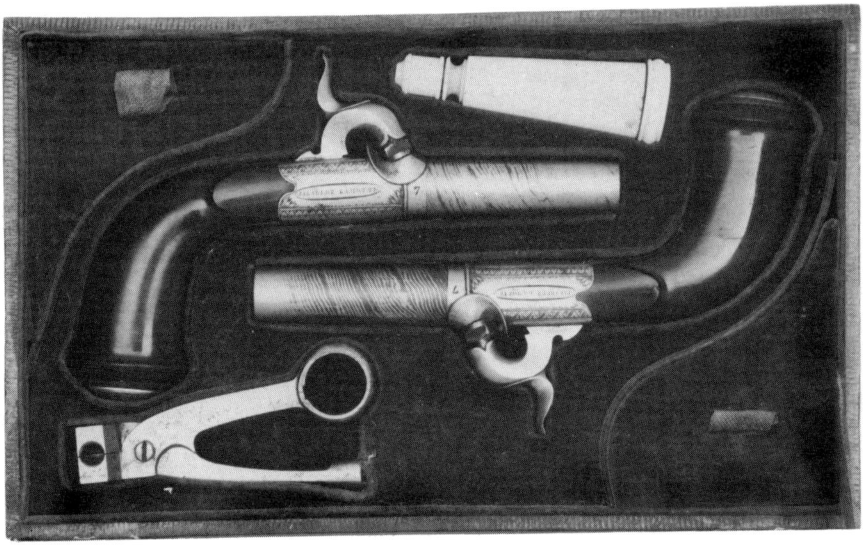

164

164. Cased pair of French percussion-cap pocket pistols, circa 1840 – unusual in having rifled barrels – contained in a velvet-lined case with ivory powder flask and combined bullet mould and ramrod.

165. A strange-looking pistol – it is in fact a fuze igniter. The brass barrel was placed over the touch hole or at the end of a fuze. When the cap was fired the flash ignited either the fuse or the main charge of powder. It is fitted with a belt hook for convenience of carrying.

166. In general, British taste favoured a frugal approach to decoration on pistols, but the French taste was for more ornate features. This cased pair of percussion-cap target/duelling pistols, circa 1860, by Lepage Frères of Paris, are fairly typical of the period and style. The rifled barrels are fluted and the locks and hammers are engraved while the ebony butts are fluted and carved. The case is velvet-lined and the compartments are contoured to the accessories. Although very decorative these sets are not tremendously popular with collectors.

167. Cased pair of percussion-cap target or duelling pistols of the mid nineteenth century. The octagonal barrels have original browning and are signed COLLINS, VIGO ST. LONDON. Apart from a missing ramrod and ramrod tip and some slight rusting the set is in very good order and condition.

168. Pair of percussion-cap duelling pistols, by Manton of London, which have octagonal barrels dating from the late eighteenth century. The stock and locks date from about 1820, but there is no reason to query the genuineness of the weapon. They were probably made to order in about 1820 and the owner or perhaps Manton felt the older barrels should be used. The case holds the correct accessories and the lid has a maker's label.

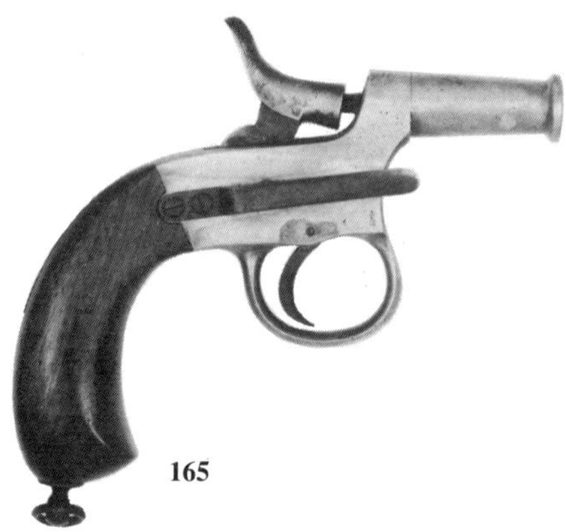

165

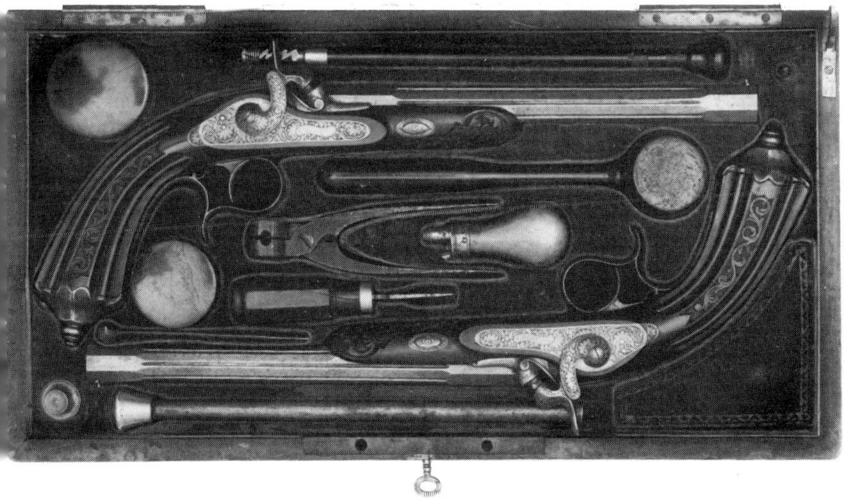

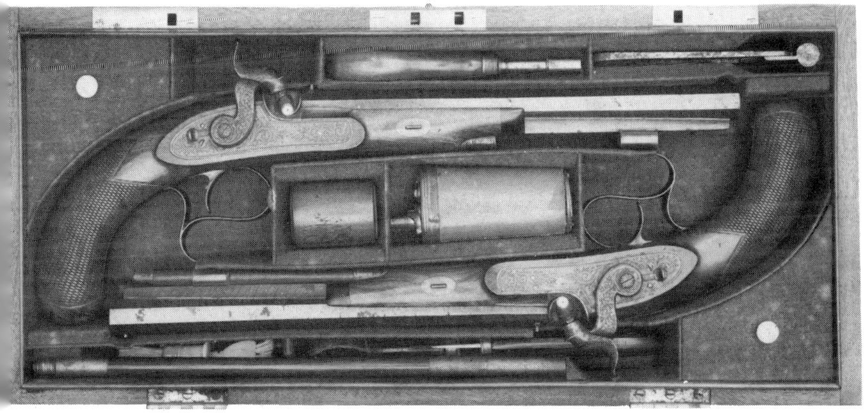

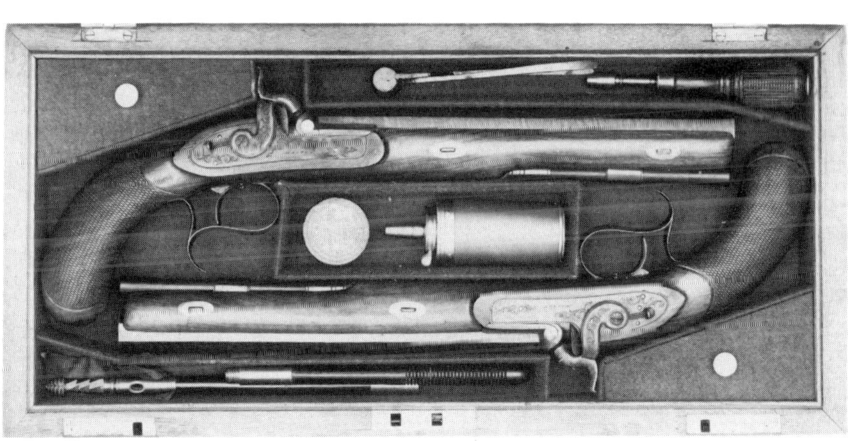

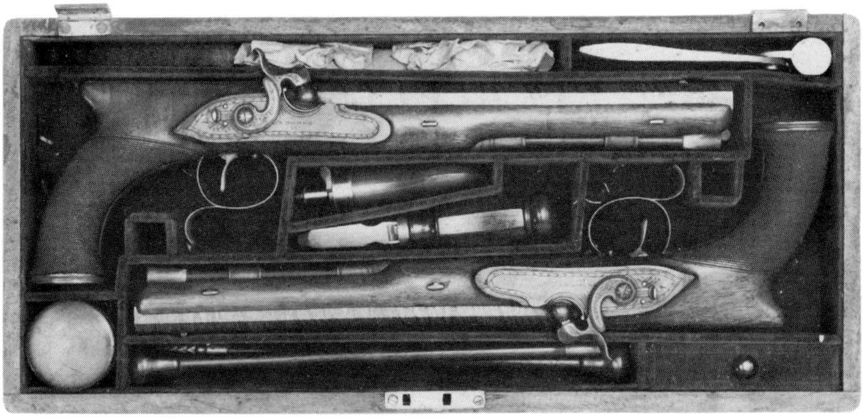

169

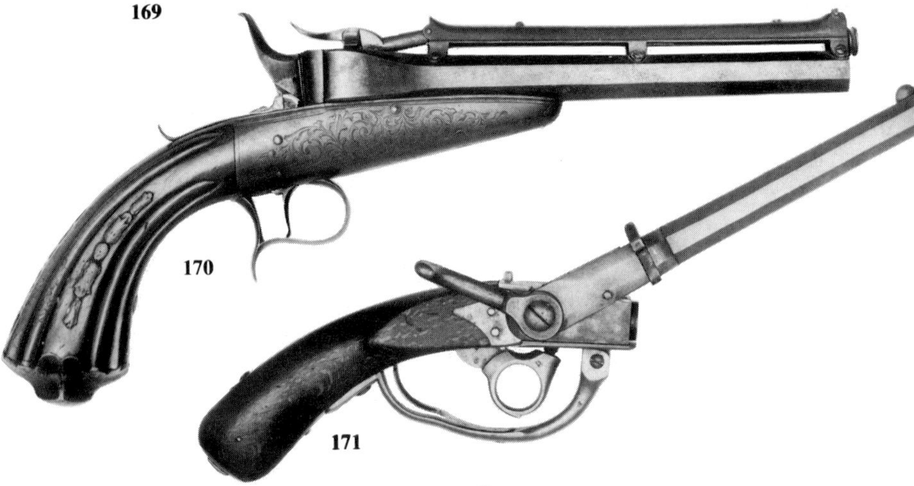

170

171

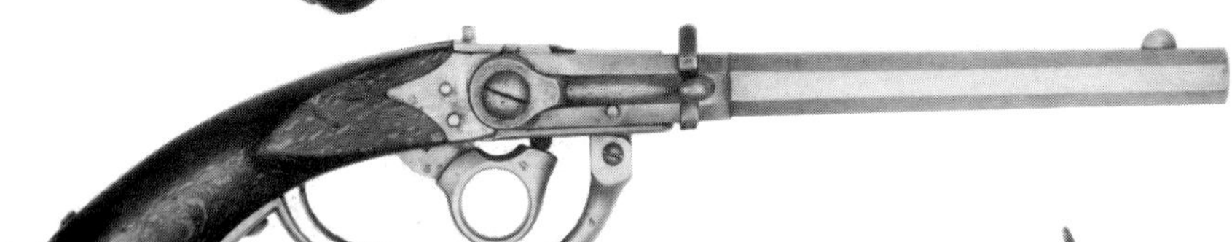

172

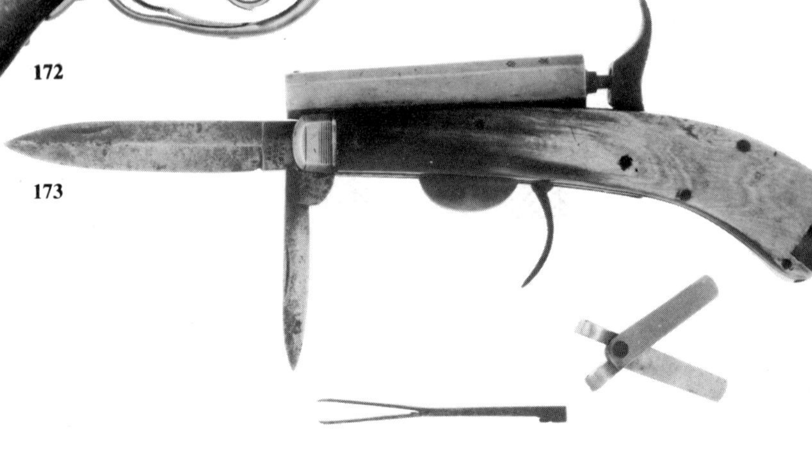

173

169. A different style of percussion-cap duelling pistol, circa 1830, by H. W. Mortimer, incorporating most of the features of the late duellers. The stocks have saw-handle butts and spurred trigger guards for a firm grip. The locks were originally flint and have push-on safety catches; the triggers can be set to operate on the lightest touch.

170. The mid nineteenth century was an active period in the gun trade with numerous attempts to increase firepower and reliability. This Belgian gravity-feed pistol was a magazine, breech-loading weapon but it was not popular. The special bullets, enclosing a charge and primer, were housed in the tube above the barrel. Cocking the hammer operated the mechanism to extract a round and load it into the breech. Rare and in good condition.

171 and 172. The leakage of gas at the breech caused a loss of power which was a major problem when designing breech-loading pistols. There were many attempts to overcome the problem and this underhammer Löbnitz pistol used a system patented in 1833 and adopted by the Danish Army in 1841. The barrel was unlocked, moved forward and pivoted upwards to allow a paper cartridge to be inserted in the breech. A cap was placed on the nipple situated beneath the frame and the barrel was then locked back in place, ready to be fired.

173. Knife pistols such as this example were popular in about the middle of the nineteenth century, and both percussion and cartridge versions were produced. This percussion specimen has an octagonal, nickel-silver Birmingham proved barrel, folding trigger, and retains its small bullet mould and combined ramrod-tweezers housed in the bone grips. Many of these pistols were produced by Unwin and Rodgers of Sheffield.

174. A Belgian pinfire revolver of late nineteenth century, with its shaped case. Its engraved frame is nickel-plated and it has a trigger which can be folded up to reduce the chance of a snag causing an accidental discharge. Now accepted by many British police forces as being antique, these pinfire revolvers have become more expensive.

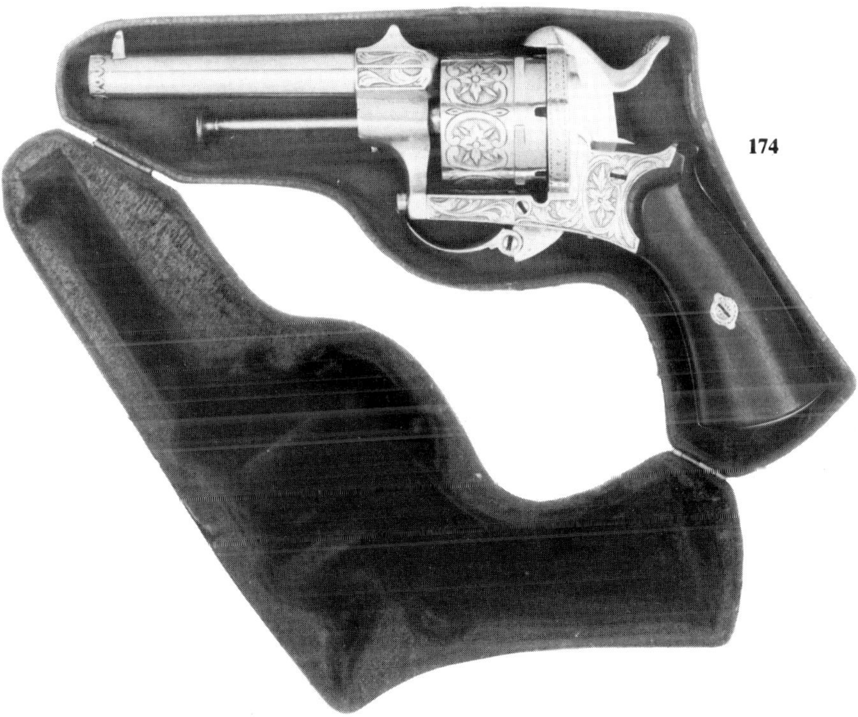

174

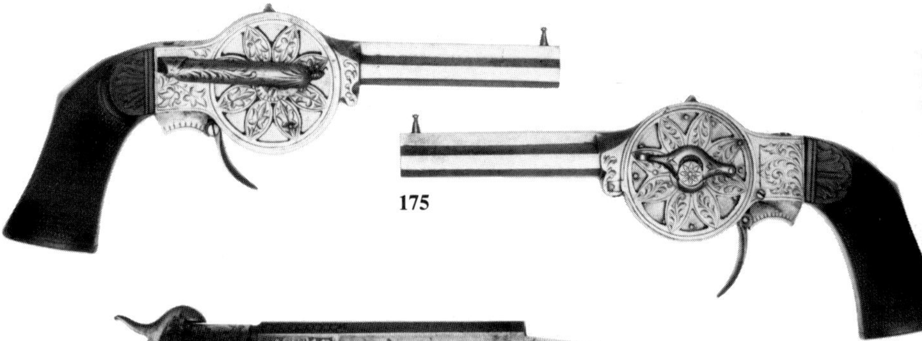

175

176

177

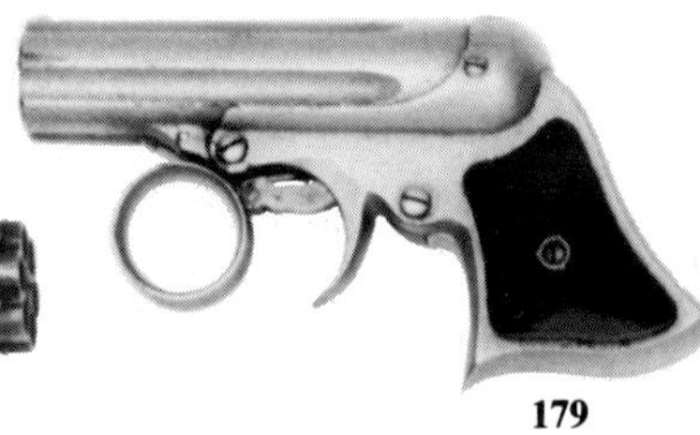

179

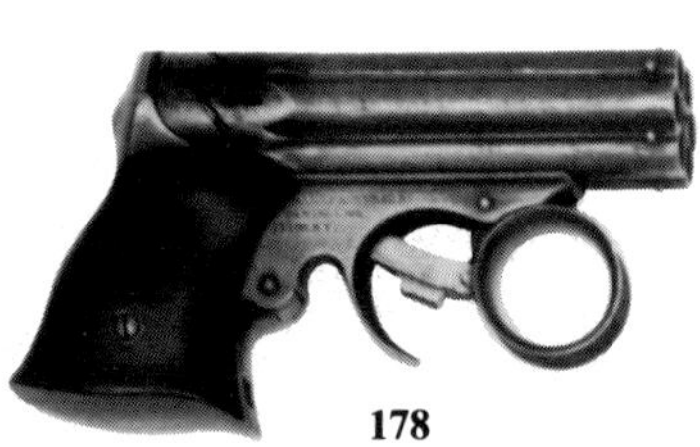

178

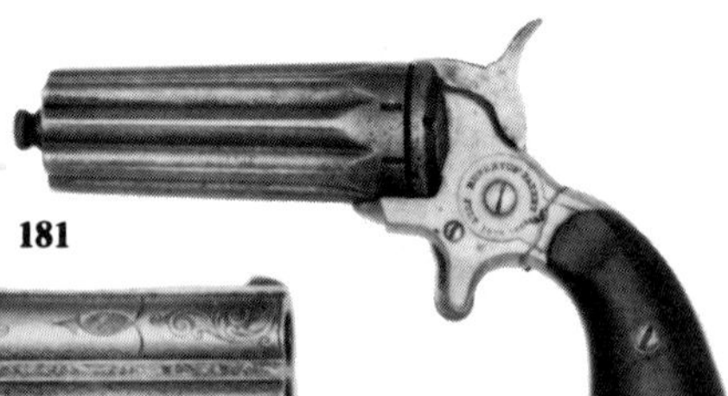

181

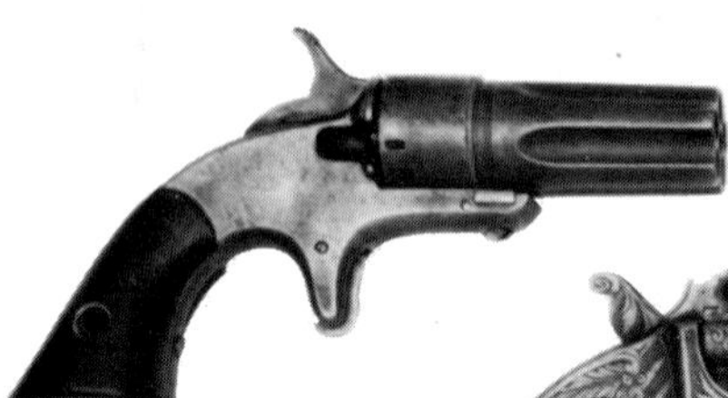

180

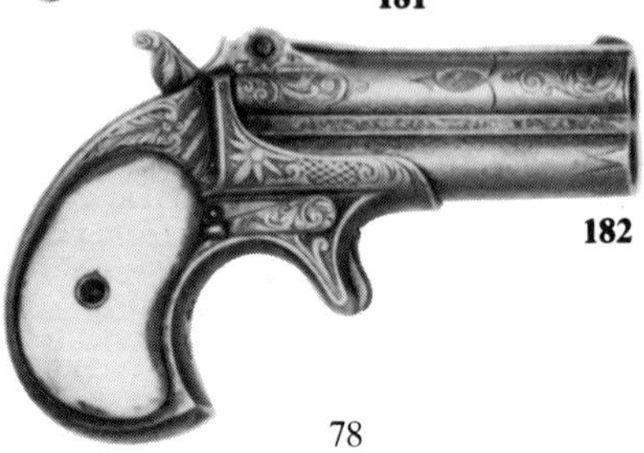

182

183

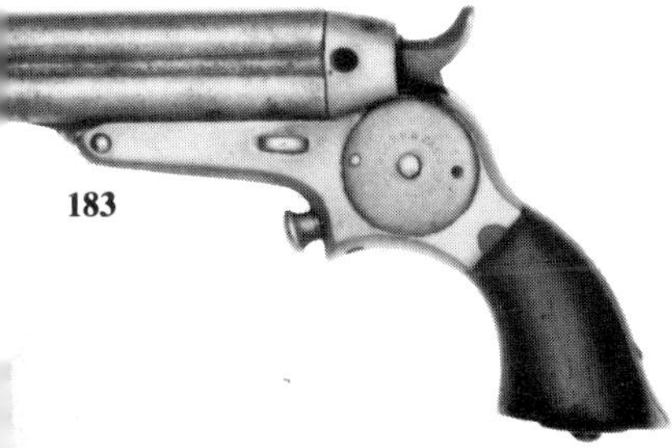

184

185

175. A pair of most unusual turret revolvers, circa 1860. The flat discs have ten radial chambers and the hammer is mounted on the outside of the disc (see upper pistol). As the folding trigger is pressed the disc is rotated, the long hammer lifted and allowed to fall to detonate the charge. The system was patented in Britain in 1865 although the original idea was devised by Sebastian Noël and François Gueury of France where it was known as a Rotovolver.

176. An 11.5mm pinfire knife revolver, circa 1870. The Bowie-shaped blade is etched with foliage and the breech section is signed DUMONTHIER. The six-chambered cylinder is also etched and has traces of gold decoration. The grips are of carved ebony.

177. A 'three-in-one' weapon. it has a six-chambered cylinder and fires a 7mm pinfire cartridge. The brass frame is fitted with a folding, sinuous blade, and the butt section is formed to serve as a knuckleduster. This type of weapon, popular in the late nineteenth century, was known as an Apache pistol after the slang name given to violent French criminals.

178. A Remington .22 Deringer, circa 1861–2. It has a six-chambered cylinder which is rotated by means of a zigzag groove at the rear.

179. Another .22 Remington Deringer, circa 1861. The frame is nickel-plated. Neither of these weapons would be considered antique in Britain and a collector would require a Firearm Certificate.

180. A 'Lady's Companion' .22 five-chambered pepperbox revolver, circa 1866 – made by Converse and Hopkins. The weapon is stamped CONTINENTAL ARMS CO. NORWICH CT. PATENTED AUG. 28 1866.

181. Another variety of .22 pepperbox revolver, this time with eight chambers. The brass frame is stamped RUPERTUS PATENT JULY 19TH 1864. RUPERTUS PAT. PISTOL MFG CO. PHILADA.

182. An over-and-under .41 Rimfire Remington Deringer of the late nineteenth century, patented in 1865. The grips are of ivory and the frame is engraved and has traces of gilding.

183. A four-barrel .30 Starr's pistol, circa 1865–70. The barrels are iron and the frame brass. In general design and appearance the pistol resembles the Sharps four-barrel pistol.

184. A .41 Rimfire Deringer, circa 1865–69, made by the National Arms Company and virtually identical with a Colt No. 2 Model.

185. A .32 four-barrel Deringer, circa 1863–88. The barrels are inscribed MANUFACTURED BY E. REMINGTON & SONS ILION, N.Y. ELLIOTS PATENTS MAY 29 1850 OCT 1 1851. It has a ring trigger such as those found on some percussion-cap pepperbox revolvers.

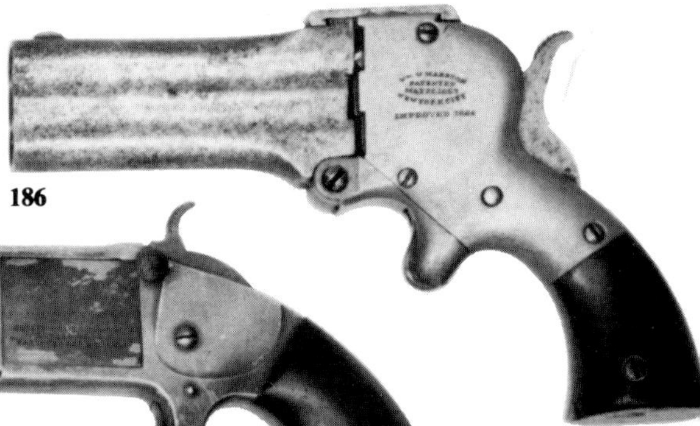

186

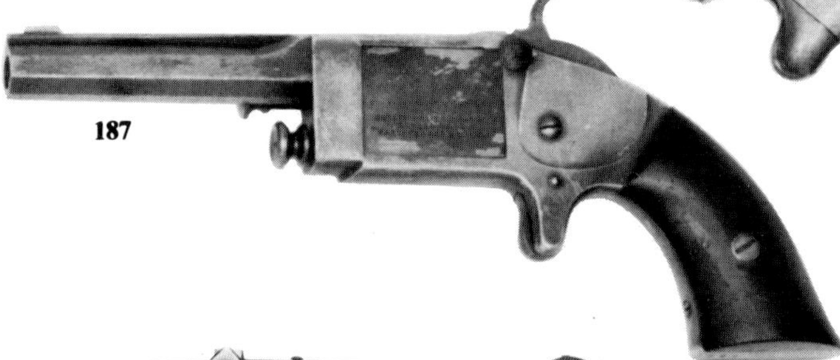

187

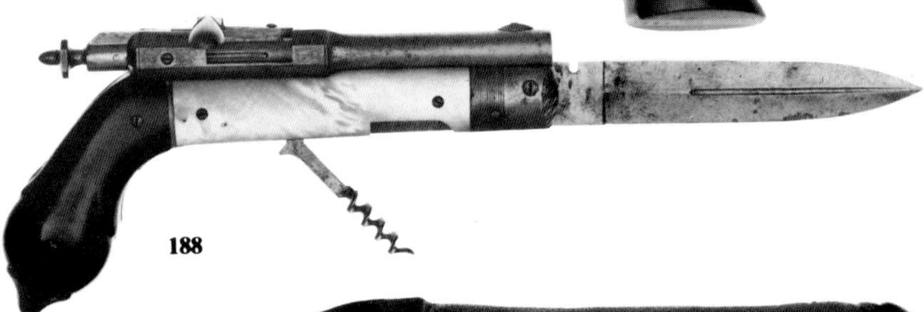

188

189

190

186. A three-barrel .32 pistol stamped WM. W. MARSTON. PATENTED MAY 26 1857 NEW YORK CITY IMPROVED 1864. The barrels are hinged at the base and pivot downwards for reloading.

187. Another .32 rimfire pistol with a pivoted breechblock which swings sideways and is stamped ROLLIN WHITE ARMS CO. LOWELL MASS. PATENTED APR. 13 1858. Rollin White was the owner of the patent for drilling through the cylinders of revolvers to allow them to accept a cartridge from the back.

188. Most unusual French, needle-fire knife pistol – mid nineteenth century. The corkscrew serves as the trigger and the pistol is loaded with a cartridge with its own internal primer which is struck by a long needle mounted on the breech. Its rarity value is enhanced by the fact that the original holster has survived.

189 and 190. Attempts to conceal pistols have been ingenious, ranging from those disguised as Japanese fans to this one in a purse. A metal-framed purse houses a small, six-shot pinfire pistol, firing through one side of the purse's frame. The idea was that an unsuspecting thief could be disposed of as the victim handed over the purse. The design was patented in Britain and the USA by Frankenau in 1877.

191. This four-barrel pistol, patented in Paris in 1866 by Biedermann, is unusual and made especially attractive by retaining its original holster. The weapon takes rimfire cartridges and each is struck, in turn, by a hammer with a rotating nose. Each time the hammer is cocked the nose rotates through 90° to bring the striker in line with the next cartridge to be fired.

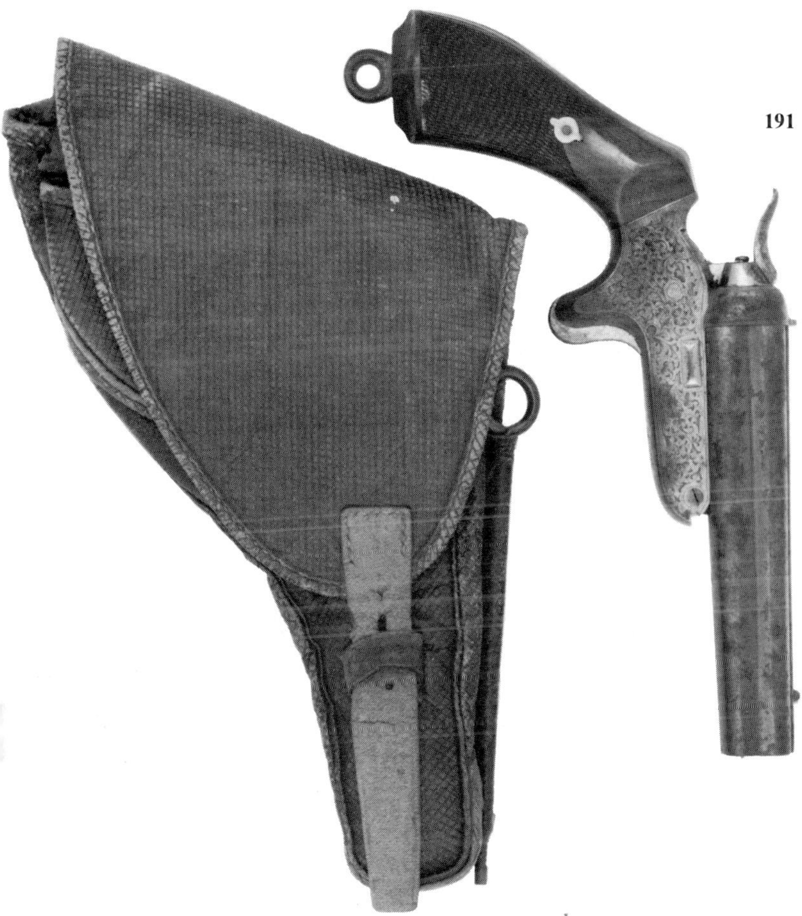

191

192

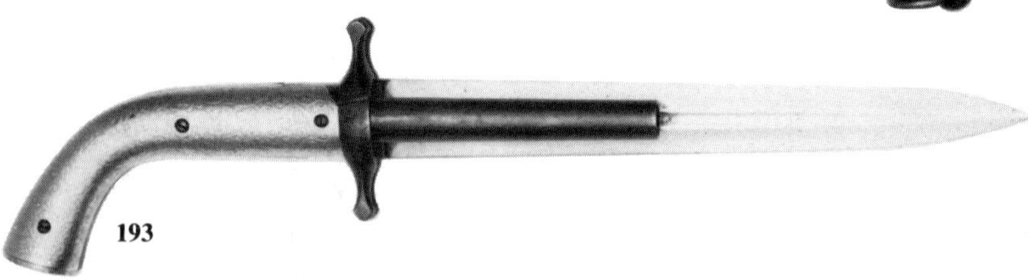

193

194

192. Some pinfire weapons of enormous firepower were produced, although handling them must have been quite a problem. This Belgian pinfire revolver, circa 1860, has a cylinder with thirty chambers. The frame is engraved with a foliate pattern and the grips are of ebony.

193. A French knife pistol of the mid nineteenth century. The double-edged blade is signed DUMONTHIER BREVET DUN and is fitted with a silver-plated hilt. A percussion-cap pistol is fitted on each side of the blade and the crossguard arms, the quillons, form the hammers.

194. A fine cased rimfire revolver in its wallet carrying case. It is difficult to date such weapons for they remained in production for a long period, but most are of the late nineteenth century. This example is nickel-plated and has ivory grips.

195

196

197

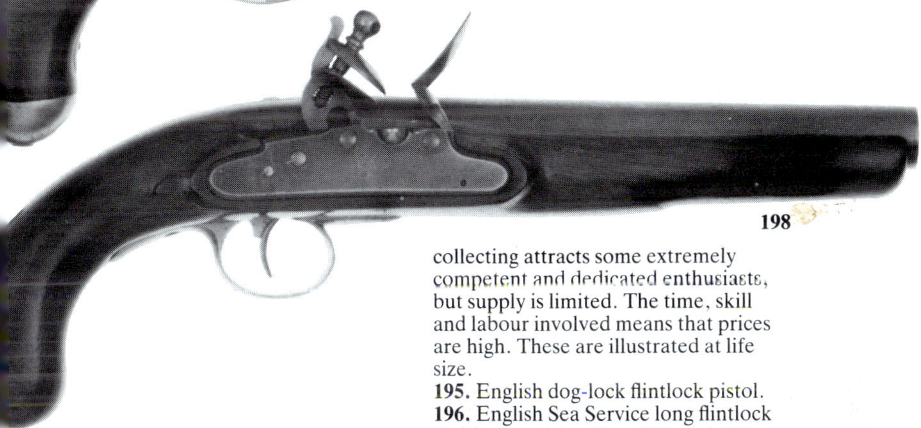

198

195 to 198. These superb miniature pistols are exact but scaled-down copies of the original weapons. This field of collecting attracts some extremely competent and dedicated enthusiasts, but supply is limited. The time, skill and labour involved means that prices are high. These are illustrated at life size.

195. English dog-lock flintlock pistol.

196. English Sea Service long flintlock pistol.

197. Austrian flintlock pistol.

198. English flintlock pistol with Nock screwless lock. (Private Collection)

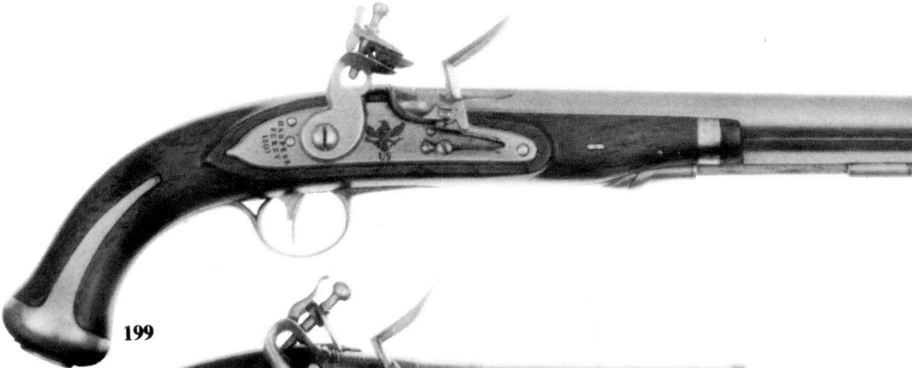

199

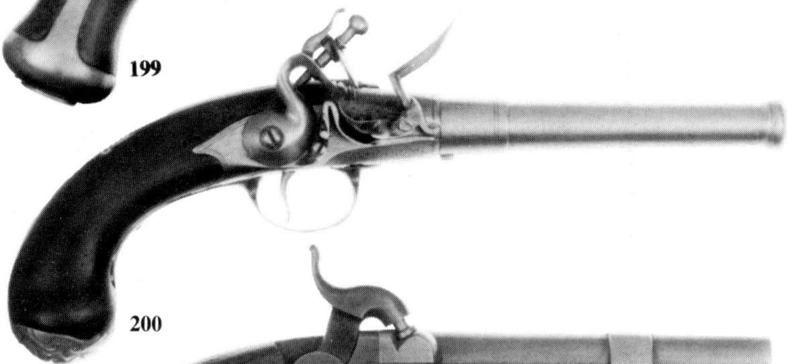

200

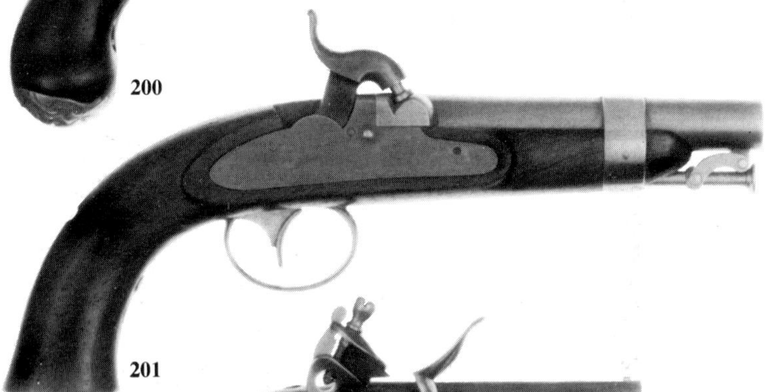

201

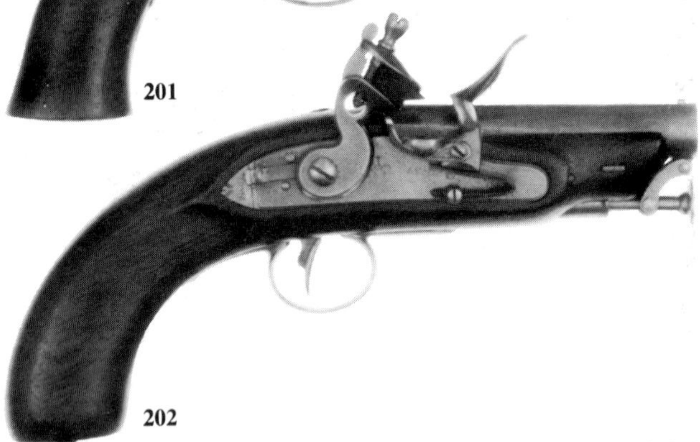

202

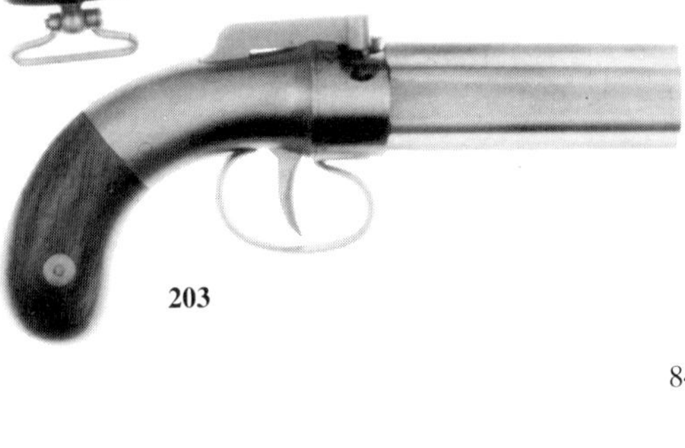

203

199 to 203. More miniature pistols, again illustrated at life size.
199. A Harpers' Ferry (USA) flintlock pistol.
200. A Queen Anne flintlock pistol.
201. An Ames Company (USA) percussion pistol.
202. British Coastguard flintlock pistol.
203. Percussion-cap pepperbox revolver. (Private Collection)